I0055609

The
EARLY
START
RETIREMENT
PLAN

"Danette Lowe offers valuable insights with thoughtful attention to detail, clarity, and wisdom. This book provides practical guidance to help readers navigate retirement with confidence and foresight."

DAVID M. DARST

CFA®, Managing Director and Chief Investment Officer, Americana Partners, and former Chief Investment Strategist, Morgan Stanley Smith Barney

"Providing tips, sharing stories, and including key takeaways at the end of chapters creates opportunities for readers to visualize and apply the concepts in their own lives. The material is engaging and also empowers readers to take actionable steps toward their retirement goals. Danette's ability to break down complex financial concepts into manageable pieces is impressive and ensures that readers from all backgrounds can benefit from her expertise."

ANGELA SARVER

EllieBlu Human Resources Consulting

"Danette hits it out of the park with this one-of-a-kind retirement book. She talks about living abroad to eco retirement adventures! It's a must-read for anyone thinking about their next chapters!"

JILL M. HANSEN

CFP®, RLP®, CLTC® - Hansen Financial MV

"Comprehensive yet accessible, *The Early Start Retirement Plan* offers a holistic perspective on retirement. This book addresses the realities and practicalities of transitioning into a retirement lifestyle—not just any lifestyle, but the one you've always dreamed of. Regardless of your current stage in retirement planning, Danette provides practical knowledge and insights on how to comfortably navigate this significant life change. I highly recommend this book to anyone over 40. However, younger readers should also consider it; there's no reason to wait. This book seamlessly lays out the next steps, empowering you to shape your retirement years to suit your personal aspirations."

CARSON McD

"Wow, what a great book! Initially, I was a bit hesitant because finances have always been tricky for me. However, I found *The Early Start Retirement Plan* incredibly helpful. The inside tip guides are so valuable. What I love the most is that I didn't feel overwhelmed. Now, I feel confident that I can sit down and create a better plan for my future. Admittedly, I haven't been the best financial planner, but your book gives me hope and the tools to do better for my future."

ELIAS PATRAS
Author of "From the Universe to Our Hearts"

"The financial resource every woman needs. Danette's book not only demystifies retirement planning by removing fear from the process, but she also infuses excitement by aligning it with your passions and values. As a career and life coach for women, I will recommend this book to all my clients to ensure they are creating an empowered financial future."

JANET ZAVALA
Author of "The Nature of Transformation"

"Danette masterfully shatters the concept of retirement as the final chapter of life and introduces us to the most inspiring chapter one could imagine. This is a book every financial advisor will be excited to place in the hands of their clients."

CHRISTY RAINES
CFP® AIF® - Azimuth Wealth Management

"Danette is a down-to-earth, master teacher on how to achieve your perfect world in retirement. Kudos to her on her new book which breaks down all the successful ways people have prepared for and moved into retirement. The case studies and real-life stories she shares are my favorite part of this book."

JANET WILSON
AIF® - Janet Wilson Wealth Management

"What a fantastic literary addition under the topic of 'retirement.' Danette has done a masterful job of organizing and articulating the myriad of possibilities in this next chapter called retirement. Enjoy!!"

SHELBY TRINKINO
CFP® - Independent Wealth Strategies

Statements were provided in August 2024 by readers, who are non-clients. This statement may not be representative of the experience of others and is not a guarantee of future performance or success.

The
EARLY
START
RETIREMENT
PLAN

*Craft a Portfolio of
Passions to Enrich Your
Life Today and Beyond*

DANETTE GAY LOWE, CFP®

PUBLISHED BY

✦ TruNorth Wealth
MANAGEMENT LLC
USA, 2024

TruNorth Wealth
MANAGEMENT LLC

First Edition

Copyright © 2024 Danette Gay Lowe
www.EarlyStartRetirement.com

All rights reserved.

ISBN: 979-8-9889813-3-6

No part of this book may be reproduced or transmitted in any form or by any means, electronic or mechanical, including photocopying, recording or by an information storage and retrieval system – except by a reviewer who may quote brief passages in a review to be printed in a magazine, newspaper or on the Web – without permission in writing from the publisher.

Cover Design & Layout by Margaret Cogswell Designs
www.margaretcogswell.com

WITH DEEPEST GRATITUDE AND LOVE

For My Mom - Your unwavering belief in me has been a guiding light throughout my life. Your encouragement and wisdom have shaped me into the person I am today, daring to dream and achieve beyond what I imagined possible.

For Derek - My steadfast partner and best friend, your constant support and love have been the bedrock of my journey. Your strength and belief in my endeavors have given me the courage to push forward, even in challenging times.

For Jake & Brian - My wonderful sons, I am immensely proud of the incredible men you have become. Jake, you have faced your challenges with such strength and grace, and your achievements and determination are nothing short of inspiring. Brian, your drive and resilience have led you to remarkable successes, and your kindness and generosity touch everyone around you. Both of you continue to amaze me with your compassion and accomplishments. Watching you grow into such admirable individuals is one of the greatest joys of my life, and your stories of perseverance and achievement inspire me every day. I love the sound when you laugh together, it warms my soul.

For Isabel and Rory - Isabel, my precious granddaughter, your joyful spirit brightens my life. Seeing the world through your eyes fills me with hope and happiness.

Rory, my grandson, I eagerly anticipate the incredible person you will grow to be. May your journey be filled with discovery, growth, and fulfillment.

For Sereah - Thank you for being a wonderful daughter-in-law and a cherished friend. Your dedication as a mother and your remarkable achievements in your studies fill me with pride. I love you dearly and am grateful for the joy you bring into our family.

For Don and Moe - My cherished parents-in-law, from the moment we met, your warmth and acceptance have been a source of comfort and strength. Your unwavering support has been a blessing throughout our lives together.

For Anna and Penelope - It's been a joy to welcome you into our lives. Your presence is a delight, and I look forward to getting to know you both better. It's wonderful to have you as part of our family, and I am excited for the memories we will create together.

For Donna - My sister, your dedication and hard work do not go unnoticed. I admire your relentless drive and the way you tackle every task with determination. Thank you for being a part of my journey.

For Leslie - My sister-in-law, your resilience in facing life's challenges is truly admirable. Your strength and determination inspire me, and I deeply appreciate having you in my life.

For Chris and Carrie - Our "new" brother and sister, it's been a joy getting to know you both. Your warmth and kindness have quickly made you a cherished part of our family. I'm grateful for the bond we're building and am excited about the many memories we'll create together.

For My Nieces and Nephew - Ashley, Bailey, Emily, Katelynn, Sydney, and Aaron: I am filled with hope and excitement for your futures. Each of you is an outstanding individual with immense potential, and I'm eager to see the incredible lives you will create for yourselves. This book is dedicated to inspiring younger people like you to take the time to truly craft a life that's rich with purpose and fulfillment.

For Uncle David, Josh, Jacob, Jonathan, & TJ - I'm so grateful to have you in my life. Your love and support mean the world to me, and I cherish the memories we've shared. I miss Karen and Loretta every day, and their spirit continues to inspire me.

For Jed - My dear friend, your wise counsel over the years has been invaluable. We've spent countless hours talking through challenges and sharing insights, often finding ourselves facing the same hurdles at the same time. Your wisdom and friendship have been a huge part of my journey, and I'm truly grateful for the way you've enriched my life both professionally and personally.

For My Diamond Dominoes - Christy, Janet, Jessica, Jill, Laura, and Shelby - my work sisters and dear friends. Your unwavering support, encouragement, and friendship mean the world to me. I am immensely proud of each of you and deeply appreciate the love and inspiration you bring into my life. Together, we've navigated challenges and celebrated victories, and I cherish every moment of our journey. Thank you for being my steadfast allies and dear friends.

For My Commonwealth Community - To my friends in
the Commonwealth Community - both those in the home office and my fellow financial advisors - your support, collaboration, and camaraderie have been truly invaluable. I deeply appreciate the connections we've built and the ways in which you've enriched my professional journey. Thank you for being a part of this journey with me.

Elias, Delora, Rose, Carson, and Janet
Elias, Delora, Rose, Carson, and Janet – You understand the power of living in the present moment and you are inspirational to me. Your presence and friendship have been a source of strength and joy. The time we spend together at retreats has been transformative, and I am deeply grateful for your wisdom and companionship.

This book is dedicated to each of you, with deep
gratitude and love for the roles you have played in my life.
You have enriched my journey immeasurably,
and I am forever grateful.

A HEARTFELT THANK YOU
TO MY CLIENTS

To my valued clients, who I cherish deeply and who have been the heart and soul of this book. Your trust, stories, and experiences have profoundly shaped the insights and guidance shared within these pages. Over the years, I have had the privilege of witnessing your resilience, growth, and triumphs, and it has been my honor to support you on your journeys.

During the recent pandemic, when the world seemed uncertain and challenging, your thoughtful messages and unwavering support were a source of great comfort. It was a time that tested all of us, and your concern for my well-being, as well as our shared moments of concern and encouragement, highlighted the strength of our relationship. These experiences reinforced the deep bond we share and reminded me of the incredible community we have built together.

I am profoundly grateful for the opportunity to be a part of your lives, to share in your milestones, and to offer support during times of need. Every day, I am inspired by your courage and dedication, and I strive to serve you with the same level of care and commitment you have shown me. Your trust in me is a treasured gift, and I am continually motivated to help you achieve your goals and navigate life's challenges with confidence.

Thank you for being such an integral part of my professional journey and for allowing me to be a part of yours. It is with heartfelt gratitude that I dedicate this book to you, my valued clients. Your support and the lessons we have learned together have made this endeavor possible, and I look forward to continuing our journey together, now and in the future.

IN MEMORY OF MY DAD

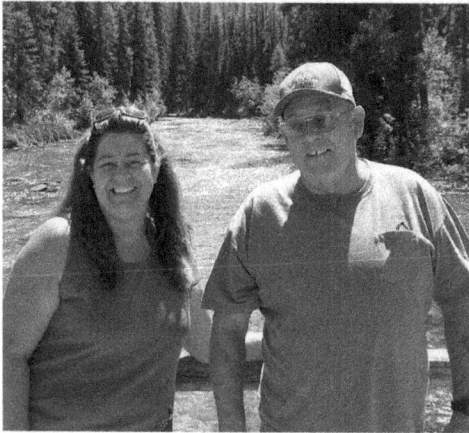

Dad, though you are no longer with us, your legacy of strength, determination, and love continues to guide me every day. I often feel your presence with me, especially when I'm working, and it's as if you're watching over me from heaven. I feel your pride in my accomplishments and carry your memory in my heart always. Your influence shapes who I am and everything I do, and I am deeply grateful for the enduring impact you've had on my life.

CHAPTER 9
Overcoming Challenges & Navigating "Life Quakes" in Retirement

CHAPTER 10
Crafting Your Personalized Retirement Plan

Introduction

Welcome to *The Early Start Retirement Plan*. Did you know that people often spend more time planning their summer vacation than they do their retirement? It's a startling statistic that underscores a common oversight. Planning for a two-week getaway is exciting and tangible, but when it comes to envisioning the decades-long journey of retirement, many feel overwhelmed and uncertain. This apprehension often leads to procrastination, leaving retirement planning on the back burner until it's almost too late.

Even more surprising, a recent study found that 42% of Americans just guess and stop working without a concrete plan. This lack of preparation can lead to unnecessary stress and financial insecurity during what should be the most enjoyable years of life. The fear of the unknown, coupled with the complexity of financial planning, can be paralyzing.

People worry about whether they've saved enough, how to manage their investments, and what their daily lives will look like without the structure of a career. This book is designed to demystify the process, breaking it down into manageable steps that make planning for retirement as engaging and rewarding as planning for that dream vacation.

Transforming Fear into Excitement and Clarity

My goal with this book is to change that narrative, to take the fear out of the planning process and replace it with excitement and clarity. The Early Start Retirement Plan aims to inspire you to start planning now, regardless of where you currently stand.

By introducing you to a variety of fulfilling and enriching activities you can incorporate into your life today, this book will help you see retirement not as an end, but as a beginning. Whether it's exploring new hobbies, pursuing lifelong dreams, or even starting a second career, you'll learn how to create a vibrant and purposeful retirement. Let's embark on this journey together, transforming apprehension into anticipation and crafting a future filled with possibilities.

Leveraging Decades of Expertise in Financial Planning

With over two decades of experience in financial planning, I've witnessed the evolving landscape of retirement. As a CERTIFIED FINANCIAL PLANNER™ practitioner, I have had the privilege of helping hundreds of families navigate the complexities of preparing for their future.

My expertise in the field has not only been honed through one-on-one consultations but also through frequent speaking engagements where I share insights on behavioral finance. This specialized area of study delves into the psychological factors that influence financial decision-making, allowing me to provide a deeper, more empathetic approach to retirement planning.

Retirement has transformed from a period of winding down to an exciting phase of life ripe with opportunities for growth, adventure, and personal fulfillment. No longer seen as merely a time to rest, retirement is now viewed as a new chapter filled with potential for pursuing passions and exploring new horizons.

However, despite this shift, many individuals approach retirement with uncertainty. Most people come to me just 2 to 3 years before they plan on retiring to see if they've saved enough. This last-minute scramble often stems from a lack of understanding about what retirement can truly offer beyond the financial aspects.

The answer to whether they've saved enough depends on what they want to do, how do they want to spend their time, and frankly, most people have no idea what's even possible. This book is here to bridge that gap. By leveraging my extensive experience and insights, I aim to help you envision a retirement that is not just financially secure but also profoundly fulfilling.

Together, we will explore the myriad of opportunities

available and craft a plan that aligns with your deepest desires. Whether it's traveling the world, starting a new business, or engaging in lifelong learning, you'll discover that the possibilities are endless. My goal is to equip you with the knowledge and confidence to start planning early, ensuring that your retirement is as vibrant and dynamic as you've always dreamed it could be.

Embrace Vibrant Experiences Today

Retirement, as we see it today, is no longer confined to leisure and relaxation. It's about embracing vibrant experiences that align with your passions, dreams, and aspirations. But why wait until retirement to start living this way? This book is designed not just as a guide for your future retirement, but as a roadmap to enrich your life now.

Imagine a life where you're actively pursuing your interests, engaging in activities that bring you joy, and building a portfolio of passions that will carry you into retirement and beyond.

By starting to participate in these types of activities now, you can begin to experience the benefits of a fulfilling, purpose-driven life today. Whether it's exploring new hobbies, volunteering for causes you care about, or investing time in lifelong learning, these experiences will not only enhance your present but also provide a solid foundation for a vibrant retirement. This proactive approach transforms retirement planning from a future concern into an immediate, joyful pursuit.

Craft a Life Resonating with Your Deepest Desires

This book is a beacon, guiding you through the diverse possibilities that modern retirement offers and encouraging you to craft a life that resonates with your deepest desires. By integrating your passions into your daily routine now, you'll find that the transition into retirement becomes a natural and exciting continuation of your current lifestyle. You'll no longer see retirement as a distant, uncertain phase of life but as an extension of the fulfilling life you're already living.

Through practical advice, inspirational stories, and actionable steps, this book will help you identify and cultivate the activities that bring you the most joy. You'll learn how to balance these pursuits with your current responsibilities, ensuring that you live each day to its fullest potential. Embracing this mindset will not only make your journey to retirement more enjoyable but will also ensure that your retirement years are filled with purpose, excitement, and personal growth.

In essence, this book is your companion in designing a life that is rich with meaning and satisfaction, both now and in the years to come. Let's embark on this journey together, embracing the present and planning for a future that truly reflects who you are and what you aspire to achieve.

Resource Center for Your Retirement Journey

To further support you on your journey, I am excited to introduce a dedicated resource center at www.EarlyStartRetirement.com. This online hub will provide additional tools, worksheets, and exclusive content to complement the insights and strategies discussed in this book.

Throughout the chapters, I will periodically reference this resource center, guiding you to valuable materials that can help you implement the concepts and plans tailored to your unique retirement vision. Visit the website regularly to stay updated with the latest resources designed to enrich your planning process and enhance your retirement experience.

. . . . ▶

Overview of Chapters: Exploring the Path to a Fulfilling Retirement

Chapter 1: Finding Purpose and Legacy

Discover the joy of finding purpose in your retirement by engaging in activities that resonate deeply with your values and passions. This chapter explores how you can establish charitable foundations or get involved in philanthropic endeavors, offering a profound sense of fulfillment and legacy. By contributing to causes you care about, you not only enrich your own life but also leave a lasting impact on your community and the world.

Chapter 2: Entrepreneurship as a Second Act

Consider entrepreneurship as a rewarding second act in your retirement. This chapter dives into the adventure of starting new ventures, whether it's launching a small business, consulting, or turning a hobby into a profitable enterprise. You'll learn how to harness your skills and experience to create a meaningful and exciting new chapter in your life, filled with opportunities for growth and innovation.

Chapter 3: Embracing New Cultures and Communities

Open the door to the enriching experience of moving to another country in retirement. This chapter highlights the benefits of embracing new cultures and communities, from the excitement of exploring unfamiliar landscapes to the personal growth that comes from adapting to different ways of life. You'll discover practical tips for making a successful transition and building a vibrant, fulfilling life abroad.

Chapter 4: Creating a Portfolio Lifestyle

Create a rich, multifaceted retirement with a portfolio lifestyle, blending various interests and activities to keep your days dynamic and engaging. This chapter provides insights into how you can mix travel, hobbies, volunteer work, and part-time employment to create a balanced and satisfying retirement. By diversifying your pursuits, you'll maintain a sense of purpose and excitement throughout this phase of your life.

Chapter 5: The Concept of Mini-Retirements

Introduce the concept of mini-retirements, a novel approach to balancing work and leisure throughout your life. This chapter explores how taking periodic breaks to pursue passions and recharge can enhance your overall well-being and satisfaction. Learn how to integrate mini-retirements into your career planning, allowing you to enjoy the benefits of retirement at various stages of your life.

Chapter 6: Sustainable, Eco-Friendly Living

Explore sustainable, eco-friendly living as part of your retirement plan. This chapter invites you to live in harmony with nature, adopting practices that reduce your environmental footprint and promote a healthier planet. From downsizing to eco-friendly homes to embracing renewable energy sources and sustainable gardening, you'll find ways to live more sustainably and mindfully.

Chapter 7: Cultural Immersion and Lifelong Learning

Celebrate the enriching journey of cultural immersion and lifelong learning in retirement. This chapter emphasizes the importance of expanding your horizons through travel, educational pursuits, and cultural experiences. By continuously seeking knowledge and engaging with diverse communities, you'll keep your mind active and your spirit vibrant.

Chapter 8: Strategic Financial Planning

Outline strategic financial planning to support these diverse paths, ensuring a solid foundation for your dreams. This chapter covers essential financial strategies, from investment planning and income management to risk assessment and estate planning. By securing your financial future, you'll have the freedom to pursue your retirement goals with confidence and peace of mind.

Chapter 9: Navigating Challenges and Transitions

Acknowledge the challenges and transitions that come with retirement, offering strategies to navigate them smoothly. This chapter addresses common obstacles such as health issues, loss of identity, and changes in social dynamics. You'll find practical advice for overcoming these challenges and maintaining a positive outlook as you adjust to your new lifestyle.

Chapter 10: Crafting a Personalized Retirement Plan

Emphasize crafting a personalized retirement plan that reflects your unique goals and values. This chapter guides you through the process of identifying your priorities, setting realistic goals, and creating a flexible plan that evolves with your needs and desires. By tailoring your retirement plan to your individual aspirations, you'll ensure a fulfilling and meaningful retirement.

Chapter 11: Embracing Freedom of Choice

Inspire you to embrace the vast freedom of choice in retirement, encouraging you to explore the myriad paths available. This chapter celebrates the limitless possibilities that come with this phase of life, urging you to think outside the box and pursue unconventional dreams. Whether it's taking up a new hobby, traveling to distant lands, or reinventing yourself in unexpected ways, you'll be empowered to design a retirement that truly reflects who you are and what you aspire to achieve.

. . . . ▶

Shattering the Conventional Script of Retirement

This book is not merely a collection of retirement strategies; it's a compilation of stories, insights, and practical advice from those who've boldly ventured into these alternative paths. Each chapter is filled with real-life examples of individuals who have redefined retirement by embracing new opportunities, pursuing their passions, and creating lives filled with purpose and excitement.

It's about shattering the conventional script of retirement, proving that this phase of life is an opportunity for reinvention, growth, and profound impact.

Through these narratives, you will see how others have navigated the challenges and embraced the possibilities of modern retirement. Their experiences will offer you valuable lessons and inspire you to envision a retirement that breaks away from the traditional mold.

Whether it's starting a new business, traveling the world, or immersing yourself in lifelong learning, these stories will show you that retirement can be a time of unprecedented personal growth and fulfillment.

As we journey into these pages together, I'll equip you with the knowledge to navigate the retirement planning process with confidence. You'll learn from the triumphs and challenges of individuals who've embraced these paths, finding inspiration in their journeys.

By seeing what's possible, you'll be empowered to create a retirement plan that is uniquely tailored to your dreams and aspirations.

Retirement planning extends beyond the numbers; it's about designing a life you love. This book is your compass, guiding you toward a retirement that's as vibrant and dynamic as you wish it to be. Let's set sail on this adventure, exploring the possibilities, and crafting a retirement that truly reflects who you are and what you aspire to achieve.

Together, we will transform retirement from a period of rest into a chapter of rejuvenation, creativity, and endless potential.

Welcome to Your Early Start Retirement Plan!
Danette ☺

CHAPTER ONE

Finding Purpose in Retirement

As the sun sets on the familiar landscape of a lifelong career, retirement dawns with a spectrum of new possibilities. The end of a traditional work life is not a quiet retreat but an invitation to embark on one of life's most significant adventures—a quest for purpose.

This chapter, like all the chapters, is full of ideas to make retirement fulfilling! We'll start by exploring how finding a purpose can boost your happiness, why giving to causes you care about can be rewarding, and specific steps to get started with charitable giving and create a legacy.

Retirement is more than the cessation of work; it's a re-invention of self. It's an opportunity to align one's deepest values with daily actions, to make a tangible difference, and to find fulfillment in new and unexpected ways. Let me help you find your way.

Guiding Tip: Purposeful Living for Health and Happiness

Research overwhelmingly points towards the benefits of staying active in retirement. Studies show that retirees who remain physically and mentally active have a lower risk of chronic diseases such as dementia, heart disease—and they enjoy a higher quality of life, greater happiness, and a more positive outlook. Of course, it is not all or nothing. The key is to find activities you enjoy and that fit your interests and physical capabilities. You will find plenty of suggestions in this book. Start by finding purpose.

Exploring the Need for Purpose in Retirement

For so many years, the rhythm of a nine-to-five job (or whatever routine you followed) provided more than just a paycheck—it offered a built-in structure, a social network, and, significantly, a sense of purpose. Retirement is often imagined as an extended vacation brimming with leisure and freedom. However, it can instead feel like a disorienting leap into the unknown.

Let's investigate why finding a new purpose is not just beneficial but crucial for a fulfilling retirement.

Guiding Tip: Keep Learning, Live Longer, Be Happier

Learning new skills and ideas fosters social connections and combats feelings of isolation. It also creates new pathways in your brain, which is very healthy for us.

A great place to start is with MOOCs – Massive Open Online Courses. You can probably find short courses on any subject you can think of, for casual interest right up to university level. They are flexible and accessible ways to explore new knowledge. This will help you to stay mentally active and engage with a global learning community, all from the comfort of your own home.

MOOCs and other open online courses are free and available to everyone. They are provided by hundreds of reputable universities, companies and other institutions, including MIT, Harvard, Berkeley, Oxford, Cambridge, etc., and Amazon (AWS), Google, Microsoft, IBM, Salesforce, Unilever, etc.

CONTINUED ON NEXT PAGE...

> ## Guiding Tip: Keep Learning, Live Longer, Be Happier
>
> ...CONTINUED FROM PREVIOUS PAGE
>
> For a curated list of educational resources and platforms that can help you continue your learning journey, I invite you to visit our resource page at www.EarlyStartRetirement.com. There, you will find detailed information on a variety of courses and learning opportunities, making it easier for you to explore new interests and expand your knowledge. This page is continually updated to ensure you have access to the most relevant and valuable resources available.

Purpose: The Heartbeat of Daily Life

In retirement, the absence of obligatory schedules can lead to a void that demands to be filled with meaning and direction. "Purpose" becomes the heartbeat of daily life; it fuels our morning motivations and shapes our daily "why." Studies have repeatedly shown that having a sense of purpose can significantly boost our mental and physical well-being. It's tied to improved cognitive function, reduced risk of disease, and even longevity. By defining a purpose beyond the workplace, retirees can infuse their days with renewed passion and vitality.

However, the transition isn't always seamless. The very freedom that retirement promises can also be its greatest challenge. Without the external demands of a job, retirees might find themselves pondering existential questions they hadn't expected. Who am I without my business card? What do I do when I no longer have to do anything?

To ease this transition, it's essential to start integrating these purposeful activities into your life well before retirement. Begin with small steps—explore new hobbies, volunteer, or take up interests that excite you. By baby-stepping into these activities now, you'll not only enrich your current life but also create a smoother, more fulfilling transition into retirement. The "Early Start" approach ensures that your journey toward retirement is a continuation of a fulfilling life already underway.

The Path Through Challenge to Purpose

The road to purpose can be as unique as your fingerprints. Some might find purpose through volunteering, others through mentorship or creative endeavors. The key is to find activities that resonate, that align with inner values, and that offer a sense of contribution.

However, this journey isn't without its hurdles. The first step often involves wrestling with the loss of a professional identity. It's about allowing oneself to grieve the passing of a familiar life stage. Next comes the daunting task of self-reflection—looking inward to uncover the sparks that could light the way to a fulfilling retirement.

It's also essential to acknowledge the external challenges.

The landscape of purpose can be filled with practical considerations such as financial stability, physical capability, and the capacity to adapt to new roles. Nevertheless, through exploration and resilience, retirees can have a life that's not about filling time but about meaningful engagement.

The Promise of a Purpose-Driven Retirement

The essence of finding purpose in retirement is about crafting a new chapter, one where success is measured not by income or accolades, but by the richness of experiences and the impact on yourself and others. It's about the journey of self-discovery, community connection, and the realization that every day presents an opportunity to add meaning to our lives.

By embracing this new concept with intentionality, you can redefine success. Instead of briefcases and working lunches, opt for experiences that are personally enriching and socially beneficial, creating a whole new spectrum of feelings. It's about making every moment count, not just to fill time, but to find joy in living a life aligned with your deepest passions and values.

My hope for you is that you begin to weave your passions into your life, no matter where you are on your journey. Don't wait for retirement to start embracing what you love. Consider dedicating two lunch hours a month to explore a new activity or passion. Even simple steps like researching and networking with like-minded individuals can be immensely rewarding.

From today forward, let your life shine brightly as you

embark on this new path, with your eyes and heart wide open to the possibilities and potential that retirement freedom brings.

Guiding Tip: Purpose in Retirement Usually Starts as a Trickle

Our sense of purpose in retirement might not be like the deafening roar of a waterfall; often, purpose starts like the gentle gurgle of a small mountain stream. The joy could come from the simple pleasure derived from tutoring local students, the visual reward of tending a community garden, or the pride of creating something new with your own hands.

This quest for purpose could well require you to step out of your comfort zone and try new experiences. It involves trial and error, patience, and an openness to change.

It's about embracing the idea that retirement is not the end of one's productive years but an opportunity to redefine productivity in more personal and impactful ways.

The Power of Charitable Giving and Foundations

As retirees embark on their post-career journey, the act of giving back through charitable work or establishing a foundation emerges as a compelling avenue to infuse their newfound freedom with profound significance. The art of philanthropy extends far beyond the simple transaction of donating; it becomes a significant force, redefining the retiree's role in society and providing a heartfelt mission that enlivens their spirit.

Philanthropy: A New Frontier in Retirement

Retirement unfolds as an expansive canvas awaiting your brushstrokes. In this phase of life, philanthropy stands tall, not merely as a means of sharing wealth but as a source of enrichment and community building. By turning your attention to the needs of others, you can harness a lifetime of skills and experiences, channeling them into causes that stir your soul. This selfless endeavor does more than impact the beneficiaries; it offers the giver a renewed sense of purpose, identity, and belonging.

Engaging in charitable work or launching a foundation presents a unique opportunity for you to leave an indelible mark on the world. It embodies your desire to contribute to the greater good. It creates a legacy that goes beyond just money and reflects personal values and hopes for the future.

Purpose-Driven Giving: The Heart Meets the Hand

For many retirees, the desire to give back is deeply rooted in the heart. But marrying this desire with strategic action is where true impact is realized. It's the hand extending from the heart to shape a better world. When retirees establish a foundation, they carve a structured pathway for their generosity, aligning their efforts with specific goals and measurable outcomes. This amplifies the impact of their philanthropy, enabling them to tackle societal issues with focus and dedication.

The stories of retirees who have trodden this path are both inspirational and instructive. Consider the retired teacher who starts a scholarship fund to empower underprivileged students, or the former executive who sets up a foundation to support innovation in sustainable agriculture. These individuals do not simply write checks; they become intimately involved in the causes they support, bringing their insight, passion, and vision to the table.

Following a Philanthropic Pathway

Establishing a charitable foundation is a venture of both heart and mind. It begins with a spark of passion, a cause that calls out to your deepest convictions. Yet, igniting that spark into a sustainable flame requires careful planning and understanding of the philanthropic landscape. Legal structures, governance, fundraising, and financial stewardship form the pillars upon which effective foundations are built.

You should consider how to structure your charitable giving to ensure its longevity. You need to become students once again, learning about tax implications, endowment management, and the regulatory environment. This knowledge is crucial in crafting a foundation that not only survives but thrives, capable of making a lasting difference in the causes you hold dear.

The Gratifying Balance of Giving

The beauty of philanthropy in retirement is found in the delicate balance between personal fulfillment and social contribution. When you give of your time, resources, and expertise, you will discover that you receive much more in return. The joy of seeing a community flourish, the gratitude of those who you helped, and the personal growth that comes from service, are the unspoken dividends of charitable giving.

Embracing the power of charitable giving and foundations unlocks a level of purpose that elevates retirement to new heights. By establishing a foundation, you become an architect of hope and a catalyst for change, ensuring your life is rich with meaning and resonance.

Establishing a Charitable Foundation

Starting a charitable foundation is like building a ship that carries your life's legacy into the future. It's a process that combines the desire to help others with careful planning. If you want to make sure your values are part of this lasting project, it's important to know both how to do it and why it matters.

Laying the Cornerstone: Vision and Mission

The inception of any charitable foundation lies in the clarity of its vision and the strength of its mission. You must embark on a journey of introspection, asking yourself what change you wish to see and what values you want to champion. Is it education, environmental conservation, or perhaps healthcare equity? The mission becomes your True North, guiding every decision and illuminating the path forward.

Blueprints and Building Blocks: Legal and Logistical Considerations

Creating a foundation is more than an act of passion; it's an exercise in diligence. You need to find your way through the legal landscape with a keen eye for detail and regulation. You must decide on the type of foundation—public charity or private foundation—and understand the implications of each. Registering the foundation, understanding state and federal laws, and obtaining tax-exempt status form the legal framework upon which the foundation will stand.

Yet, the logistics extend beyond legalities. It's about setting up a board of trustees who share your vision and possess the commitment to carry the torch. It's about creating bylaws that serve as the rulebook for the foundation's operations, ensuring that every step taken is a step toward the greater good.

The Heart of the Matter: Governance and Structure

With the legal framework in place, you must then construct the heart of the foundation—the governance and structure. This process is a delicate dance between control and delegation. You must assemble a team that not only understands the mission but can also bring diverse skills and perspectives to the table. It's about establishing committees, defining roles, and creating a decision-making process that reflects your ethos.

Governance also means transparency and accountability. It's about developing policies for conflict of interest, ethical guidelines, and financial oversight. Each policy acts as a safeguard, ensuring that the foundation's operations remain true to your mission and transparent to its supporters and the public at large.

Cultivating Growth: Funding and Sustainability

A charitable foundation's breath of life is its funding. You need to formulate a financial strategy that ensures sustainability. This could mean an initial endowment, fundraising plans, or a mix of both. It involves financial acumen—understanding investment strategies that will grow the foundation's assets while funding its activities. A sustainable foundation is one that balances prudent financial management with ambitious charitable goals.

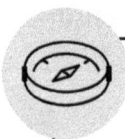

Guiding Tip: From Dream to Reality

The process of establishing a charitable foundation is indeed complex, but it is far from insurmountable. Take it step by step. Enjoy the journey from the dream of making a difference to the reality of tangible impact.

CONTINUED ON NEXT PAGE...

Guiding Tip: From Dream to Reality
...CONTINUED FROM PREVIOUS PAGE

It will be a testament to your dedication to the causes that stir hearts. It is a leap of faith supported by the pillars of careful planning and legal precision. In this way, you define your legacy in society, ensuring that your retirement is not an end but a vibrant new beginning. The establishment of a charitable foundation becomes your beacon, shining brightly as a symbol of hope, action, and enduring impact.

Balancing Financial Sustainability with Social Impact

Starting a charitable journey in retirement is a wonderful way to give back. But as you dive into making a difference, an important question arises—how do you balance your financial needs with your desire to help others? Finding this balance is key to creating a successful and lasting impact.

First, assess your financial situation to ensure you can comfortably support your lifestyle while contributing to causes you care about. Set a budget for your charitable activities, just as you would for any other expense. This helps you stay generous without jeopardizing your financial security.

Next, consider starting small. Volunteering your time or

donating smaller amounts can make a big difference and allows you to gradually increase your involvement as you become more comfortable.

Finally, seek advice from financial advisors or join groups of like-minded individuals who are also embarking on philanthropic efforts. They can offer valuable insights and help you navigate the challenges of balancing financial sustainability with your social aspirations. By taking these steps, you can make a meaningful impact while ensuring your own well-being.

The Currency of Generosity: Financial Sustainability

At the heart of any sustainable philanthropic venture lies a robust financial foundation. Retirees must navigate this terrain with the foresight of a seasoned strategist, ensuring that the wellspring of their generosity does not run dry. It starts with a solid financial plan that factors in personal living expenses, anticipated life spans, and the inevitable uncertainties of the future.

Financial sustainability in the context of charitable giving is a mosaic crafted from various income streams—pensions, savings, investments, and perhaps ongoing earnings from part-time work or a previous business. The art lies in harmonizing these streams into a symphony that plays the melody of long-term sustainability without compromising the chorus of immediate impact.

Harmonizing Impact with Intent: The Alignment of Values and Investments

Guiding Tip: A Budgeting for Both Worlds

I cannot overstate the importance of an effective budget. A comprehensive cash-flow based budget that incorporates both personal and charitable activities can serve as a roadmap. It must account for the operational expenses of the foundation and include projections for growth and potential setbacks. Moreover, a well-planned budget acts as a guide, helping to prevent overextension and ensuring the foundation's initiatives are not hindered by financial shortfalls.

Financial sustainability extends beyond mere numbers; it encompasses aligning your investments with your values and the mission of your foundation. This is where socially responsible investing (ESG) comes into play—a form of investing that considers both financial return and social and environmental good to bring about positive change.

As you embark on your philanthropic journey, you have the opportunity to ensure your investments are working for you in more ways than one. By choosing ESG investments, you can support companies and initiatives that reflect your values, thereby amplifying your foundation's mission with each invested dollar. This approach not only helps achieve your financial goals but also contributes to a better world, making your charitable efforts even more impactful.

Encore: Adapting for Sustainability and Impact

As the landscapes of economy and society shift, so too must the strategies for balancing financial sustainability with social impact. Regularly review your financial plans and investment portfolios and monitor your foundation's activities to make informed decisions and adapt as necessary. In shaping your "Loving Legacy," harmonize financial prudence with heartfelt generosity, crafting a balance that not only persists but also prospers. This enduring legacy will inspire, and effect change long after you've moved on.

Case Studies and Real-Life Stories

Within the quiet sanctuaries of retirement, some find not an end but a beginning—a renaissance of purpose through the act of giving. Their narratives unfold in communities and across continents, where the ripples of their generosity form waves of change. This section highlights the stories of individuals who have elegantly intertwined their later years with philanthropy, creating "loving legacies" that shine as beacons of inspiration.

Transforming Education: One Book at a Time

Megan, a retired elementary school teacher has made a significant impact on her community through her dedication to education and her innovative approach to fundraising.

After retiring, Megan channeled her passion for teaching into a new venture by forming a 501(c)(3) foundation aimed at enriching the classroom experience for students. Drawing on her background as a Teacher of the Year, she created a unique program where children write and illustrate their own books, which are then sold to parents, friends, and family members. This initiative not only fosters creativity and literacy but also raises much-needed funds for classroom resources.

In its inaugural year, Megan's program was implemented in just one classroom. However, its success quickly grew, and by last year, it had expanded to nine classrooms. This remarkable growth reflects both the program's effectiveness and Megan's unwavering dedication to improving educational outcomes for children.

To learn more about Megan and her inspiring work, visit www.EarlyStartRetirement.com. Her efforts have provided invaluable support to students and teachers alike, ensuring that classrooms are well-equipped, and that learning remains engaging and fun. Megan's story is a testament to the lasting impact that one dedicated educator can have, both during their career and in retirement.

The Art of Adaptability: Robert's Quest

Robert, a retired engineer, embarked on a different kind of project after his career: tackling water shortages. Robert's travels had exposed him to the harsh reality of water-deprived communities. Driven by the desire to apply his problem-solving skills, he started a small initiative to develop affordable water filtration systems using nanotech. His journey was not without obstacles; funding was limited, and technological challenges were frequent. However, Robert's tenacity and willingness to adapt his approach led to partnerships with larger non-profits, amplifying his impact and ensuring the sustainability of his efforts.

His story is a vivid illustration of how perseverance and a willingness to pivot are essential for retirees aiming to make a difference. Robert's story also underlines the importance of partnerships and collaboration in enhancing the scale and sustainability of philanthropic projects.

Cultivating Growth: Lessons Learned

Their stories teach us valuable lessons—the importance of leveraging personal strengths, the necessity of adaptability, and the strength of collective effort. These case studies shine a light on the diverse ways retirees can find purpose by serving others. They remind us that with careful planning, a generous heart, and an adaptable spirit, the journey into retirement can transition from a personal milestone to a communal triumph.

Navigating Your Philanthropic Journey with Donor Advised Funds

As you chart the course of your retirement and consider ways to leave a lasting impact, Donor Advised Funds (DAFs) can be a valuable tool in your philanthropic journey. Think of DAFs as a compass that helps guide your charitable giving, allowing you to support causes that align with your passions and values.

A Donor Advised Fund is a philanthropic vehicle established at a public charity. It allows you to make a charitable contribution, receive an immediate tax deduction, and then recommend grants from the fund over time. This flexibility makes DAFs an excellent option for those who wish to strategically navigate their charitable giving without the administrative burdens of running a private foundation.

DAFs are particularly beneficial for individuals who want to:

Maximize Tax Benefits: Contributions to DAFs are eligible for an immediate tax deduction, allowing you to reduce your taxable income while supporting your favorite causes.

Simplify Giving: By consolidating your charitable donations into one fund, you can streamline your giving process and easily manage multiple grants to different organizations.

Plan for the Future: DAFs enable you to create a strategic plan for your charitable giving, allowing you to distribute funds over several years. This ensures that your philanthropic impact continues well into your retirement journey.

Involve Family: DAFs provide an excellent opportunity to involve family members in your charitable activities, fostering a legacy of giving that can be passed down through generations.

As you embark on this exciting chapter of your life, consider how a Donor Advised Fund can serve as a navigational tool, guiding you toward meaningful and impactful philanthropy. For more information and resources on incorporating DAFs into your retirement plan, visit www.EarlyStartRetirement. com. Let's set sail on this journey together, creating a retirement that is as generous and fulfilling as you envision.

Practical Tips for Crafting a Purpose Driven Retirement Plan

As the horizon of retirement dawns, it brings with it the space for reflection and the time for action. Crafting a purpose-driven retirement plan isn't just about how you'll fill your days, but more profoundly, how you'll enrich your life and the lives of others. Here's how you can chart the course for a fulfilling retirement.

Discovering What Resonates

Begin by taking a stroll down the garden of your life, plucking memories, and passions that have always brought you joy and fulfillment. Whether it's a cause you've always cared about or an activity that ignites your spirit, let these be the seeds from which your retirement plan grows.

- Reflect on your values: follow those you hold dear. Consider how they might translate into actions or causes you want to support.

- List your passions: What sets your heart ablaze? Whether it's art, education, environmental conservation, or social justice, identify your passions. Retirement is your chance to turn them up to full flame.
- Assess your skills: Retirement doesn't mean you've left your skills behind. They're tools you can wield in new, meaningful ways. Consider how you might use them in volunteer work, mentoring, or as part of a community initiative.

Researching and Aligning with Causes

With your values and passions as your compass, embark on a voyage of discovery to find the causes that align with your inner calling.

- Educate yourself: Explore the depths of causes that interest you. Read, attend seminars, talk to experts, and embrace online sources. Knowledge will be the map that guides your journey.
- Volunteer: Test the waters by volunteering. It's a firsthand look at what's involved and a chance to see if there's a true connection.
- Network: Connect with like-minded individuals and organizations. Networking is the wind in your sails, propelling you forward and opening doors to opportunities.

Involving Your Circle

A journey is always more rewarding when shared. Involving your family and loved ones not only enriches the experience but also helps in building a support system that will sustain you.

- Discuss your plans: Share your vision with your loved ones. Their support can be the anchor that keeps you steady.
- Encourage participation: Invite them to join you in your philanthropic endeavors. It can strengthen bonds and create shared memories.
- Consider your legacy: Think about how your actions can influence the next generation. Instilling the value of giving back can be one of the most precious legacies you leave behind.

Reaping the Rewards

As you step into this new chapter, take time to celebrate the milestones, no matter how small. Each achievement is a testament to your purpose and the impact you're making.

- Document your journey: Keep a journal of your experiences. It's not just a record; it's a story of your meaningful retirement.
- Share your story: Inspire others by sharing your journey. Your story could be the beacon that lights someone else's path.
- Savor the moments: Take pleasure in the process. The joy is as much in the giving as it is in seeing the fruits of your efforts.

Purpose-driven planning can help align your actions with your values and passions, while involving your loved ones, and meeting challenges with resilience. As a result, retirement can be an enriching new beginning for you and for the world you touch.

Overcoming Challenges and Celebrating Success

In retirement, the search for purpose can sometimes feel like sailing against the wind. Challenges are inevitable, but they are also surmountable. And when you overcome them, the victories, both grand and small, deserve celebration. Here's how to navigate through the rough patches and embrace the triumphs along your journey.

Anticipating the Swells

Life's waters are rarely calm, and retirement is no exception. Anticipate the swells and know that they are a part of the course to finding purpose.

- Expect to face obstacles: Understand that challenges such as loss of identity post-career or the daunting nature of starting anew can arise. Acknowledging these potential hurdles is the first step in overcoming them.
- Adapt to the new rhythm: Retirement can change the daily rhythm you've been accustomed to for decades. Allow yourself to adapt to this new pace of life. It's not a race; it's a journey.
- Deal with uncertainty: Transitioning to a life of purpose

post-career can bring uncertainty. Lean into it. Sometimes, the most rewarding paths are the ones not yet charted.

Strategies for Navigating Setbacks

Setbacks are not full stops; they're commas in the narrative of your life, indicating a pause, a moment to recalibrate.

- Stay connected: Build a network of peers who are also navigating retirement. Shared experiences can provide comfort and solutions.
- Educate and re-educate: Embrace lifelong learning. Whether it's taking classes, attending workshops, or online, keep your mind sharp and engaged.
- Be patient with yourself: Give yourself the grace to grow into your new life. Patience is not about waiting passively; it's active perseverance.

As you sail into this next phase of life, may your challenges be met with courage and your successes with jubilation. Embrace the ebbs and flows, and remember, every chapter written, every hurdle crossed, and every success achieved is a part of your remarkable story. Your retirement isn't just a time in your life; it's a space for fulfillment, growth, and impact—a canvas still rich with possibility.

Guiding Tip: Finding Joy in the Journey

Remember, finding purpose in retirement is as much about the journey as it is about the destination.

- Enjoy the process: Revel in the learning, the community, and the sense of achievement that comes with each step forward.
- Reflect often: Regular reflection can provide deep satisfaction and reaffirm that you are living a life aligned with your values.

Stay present. Live in the moment. The joy of retirement is not just in the endpoint but in the experiences along the way.

Starting Now – Charitable Giving

From the outset of my career, I was passionate about empowering young women to pursue business education. Although establishing a full-fledged scholarship fund was part of my long-term vision for retirement, I didn't wait to start making an impact. Initially, I connected with an organization that shared my mission and contributed donations to support their scholarships. This early involvement was a practical step that aligned with my larger goal, allowing me to contribute within my means at the time.

As my career progressed, my commitment deepened. I joined the board of the local American Business Women's Association (ABWA) and played a pivotal role in their annual scholarship fundraiser. These experiences enriched my understanding of philanthropic work and prepared me for the eventual realization of my dream. Today, my firm, TruNorth Wealth Management, sponsors a scholarship at the local high school, directly supporting aspiring business students. This journey illustrates how starting small and early can lead to fulfilling your long-term aspirations, demonstrating that you don't have to wait until retirement to begin living purposefully and making a difference.

Your Reflections to Begin: Charitable Giving

1. What causes are you most passionate about, and how can you begin supporting them now, even in a small way?
2. Reflect on your long-term philanthropic goals. What steps can you take today to start moving towards these goals?
3. Can you identify organizations or groups that align with your charitable interests? How might you engage with them to contribute to your community?
4. What skills or resources do you currently have that can be utilized to make a difference in your chosen cause?
5. How can your current professional and personal networks support your philanthropic efforts, and how can you start engaging them now?

· ▶

Key Takeaways

As we close this chapter, let's reflect on the journey we've embarked upon. Finding purpose in retirement is a multifaceted pursuit, blending introspection with action, passion with planning, and individual fulfillment with communal benefit. Here are the key takeaways:

- **Aligning Retirement with Philanthropy:** Discover the joy of contributing to the greater good and building an enduring legacy.
- **Balancing Practicalities and Financial Considerations:** Learn the steps to establish a foundation and manage your finances effectively.
- **Overcoming Challenges and Celebrating Triumphs:** Navigate the ups and downs of a fulfilling retirement journey.

Let this chapter be your beacon as you navigate the expansive seas of retirement. May the stories inspire you, the strategies guide you, and the tips empower you to carve out a retirement filled with purpose, joy, and impact. Remember, the journey towards a purpose-driven retirement is best shared with others, enriched by experiences and collective wisdom.

In the chapters that follow, we will continue to build upon these foundations, exploring how life after a career can be as enriching as the years that preceded it. The road ahead is yours to shape. Welcome to your purpose-driven retirement.

CHAPTER TWO

Entrepreneurship as a Second Act

As discussed, the retirement landscape has shifted dramatically over the years. Today, retirement is no longer seen as an endpoint; it's a fresh beginning—a second act filled with promise, purpose, and the opportunity for entrepreneurial adventure. I want to take you on a journey to explore the compelling allure of entrepreneurship as a post-retirement endeavor. We'll explore the motivations that lead retirees to embark on new business ventures in their later years, revealing how entrepreneurship can offer a vibrant sense of purpose and fulfillment, and dive into the "second act" of retirement, highlighting its promising advantages.

The Appeal of Entrepreneurship in Retirement

Retirement isn't merely an end—it's a gateway to new beginnings. Many retirees turn lifetime skills into second careers by embracing entrepreneurship. This path offers a sense of accomplishment and the chance to pursue passion projects that are both fulfilling and financially rewarding.

Guiding Tip: Pioneering Your Future

Embracing entrepreneurship in your retirement years, or even sooner, isn't merely about launching a business—it's about sculpting a life enriched with purpose and passion. This phase offers a unique chance to leverage your wealth of experience, transforming long-held passions into meaningful ventures. It's an opportunity to design the future you've always envisioned, guided by the wisdom and skills honed over a lifetime.

Consider beginning now, cultivating what many refer to as a "side hustle," this approach allows you to gradually build a business that offers not only potential financial returns but also personal fulfillment and a lasting impact.

Starting small can lead to substantial achievements, turning your retirement years into a time of vibrant innovation and continued contribution, redefining the essence of retirement in your "Early Start Retirement Plan."

In my experience, I've seen numerous clients find new purpose and joy in post-retirement ventures. Entrepreneurship meets a deep-seated need for continued engagement and contribution. Starting a business allows retirees to leverage their knowledge and experience in meaningful ways.

It's about more than just staying active; it's a pursuit of passion that enriches lives. This journey brings a rejuvenation of spirit and a powerful sense of autonomy. The flexibility of entrepreneurship lets you balance work with leisure, travel, and family time.

Entrepreneurship in retirement offers continuous learning and growth. Applying a lifetime of skills in new contexts keeps the mind sharp. Starting a business can also provide financial benefits, supplementing retirement savings or turning a passion into income.

Moreover, entrepreneurship allows for positive contributions to your community or society at large. Offering valuable services, creating jobs, or supporting charitable causes leaves a lasting legacy. Embrace this "second act" as a bold step toward a fulfilling and autonomous retirement, filled with joy and personal growth.

Identifying Business Opportunities

Identifying viable business opportunities is obviously central to embarking on entrepreneurship. The key to success lies in aligning potential business ventures with personal skills, interests, and the current market demand. Here's how you can navigate this exciting phase of your entrepreneurial journey.

The first step in identifying business opportunities is introspection. You should consider your hobbies, past professional experiences, and passions. This personal inventory can reveal unique skills and interests that may form the basis of a successful business. For instance, if you have a passion for woodworking, you might consider starting a custom furniture business, or if you have a background in education, you could explore tutoring or educational consulting.

> ### Guiding Tip: Your Skills, Your Business
>
> Reflect on your lifetime of skills and interests. Your next business idea might just be hidden in your personal treasure trove of experiences.

Understanding market trends and identifying gaps are essential for ensuring the viability of any business idea. You can leverage various methods to research the market. Utilize online platforms, industry reports, and market analysis sites to gather insights into current trends and future projections. Social media and online forums can also provide firsthand accounts of consumer needs and gaps in the market.

Conduct surveys or informal conversations with potential customers to understand their needs, preferences, and the problems they face. This direct feedback can highlight unmet needs in the market that your business could address.

Engaging with individuals within your industry through

networking events, online communities, or local business groups is invaluable. These connections can provide crucial insights into the market and highlight potential opportunities. Your personal network—friends, family, former colleagues, and community members—also plays a critical role. They are excellent resources for brainstorming business ideas and understanding the needs of the market.

Additionally, I recommend reading Design Your Life by Bill Burnett & Dave Evans. The authors emphasize the importance of having "informational social conversations" with people in your community. These interactions can help you explore and understand your options as you navigate this new chapter. Their strategies are particularly relevant for anyone looking to transition into entrepreneurship after retirement, offering a structured approach to rethinking your path and aligning it with your passions and goals.

Analyze what existing businesses in your potential market are offering. Identifying services or products that are lacking can point you toward a niche you could successfully fill.

Consider scalability and sustainability as you explore different business ideas. Some ventures may start as small, passion-driven projects but have the potential to grow into larger businesses. Others might fill a niche market, providing steady income and personal satisfaction for years to come.

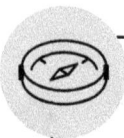

Guiding Tip: Market Insight is Key

Immerse yourself in thorough market research to truly understand what people need and desire.

Often, the most successful business ideas stem from solving a problem that you have personally encountered in your own experiences. By identifying these gaps and addressing them effectively, you not only fulfill a market need but also leverage your unique insights, enhancing the potential for your business to thrive. This approach not only helps pinpoint viable opportunities but also ensures your venture is deeply rooted in genuine personal and community needs.

Real-Life Success Stories

Drawing inspiration from retirees who turned unique business niches into successful ventures can provide valuable insights:

- Louise Hay started Hay House Publishing in 1984 when she was 58 years old. She founded the company to self-publish her book You Can Heal Your Life, which later became a bestseller and helped establish Hay House as a leading publisher in the self-help and personal development fields.

- Vera Wang embarked on her journey as a wedding dress designer at the age of 39, following a pivotal career moment when she didn't secure the top design position at Ralph Lauren. Today, she stands as one of the world's most renowned wedding dress designers, illustrating the power of pursuing one's passion regardless of age or circumstance.

- At the age of 52, Ray Kroc partnered with the McDonald brothers, taking a pivotal role in transforming a local restaurant into the global McDonald's empire we know today. His journey exemplifies how it's never too late to embark on a transformative venture and leave a monumental legacy.

- Anita Mahaffey started Cool-jams, a company that sells comfortable sleepwear, at the age of 58. She was inspired to start the business after struggling to find comfortable pajamas for herself.

- Jaleh Bisharat co-founded NakedPoppy, a clean beauty brand, at the age of 59. She was inspired to start the business after her own experiences with finding safe and effective beauty products.

These success stories highlight the limitless potential for you to identify business opportunities, based on your passion and experience, and use them to create thriving ventures.

Guiding Tip: Test Before You Invest

Embarking on a new business venture is exciting, but it's crucial to approach it with a blend of passion and pragmatism. "Test Before You Invest" encapsulates the essential first step in transforming your entrepreneurial dream into reality. This mantra emphasizes the importance of validating your business concept before committing significant resources. Conducting a thorough market analysis, understanding your target audience, and evaluating the competitive landscape are pivotal.

These steps will not only refine your business idea but also illuminate the path to a sustainable and profitable venture.

Taking the time to test your idea also minimizes risk and maximizes potential for success. It allows you to gather valuable insights, adapt your strategy, and ensure there's a market need for your product or service. This preliminary phase lays a strong foundation, helping you make informed decisions and strategize effectively. In essence, "Test Before You Invest" is about investing in your success by ensuring your business is viable, relevant, and poised for growth.

Evaluating Your Business Idea for Retirement

When you have an idea, the next step is a feasibility study to help ensure the likelihood of long-term success. Market research is crucial; identify your target audience and their needs, and analyze competitors to carve out your Unique Selling Proposition (USP).

Financial planning is essential. Create a detailed budget, estimate your Return on Investment (ROI), and establish a timeline for profitability. Develop strategies for managing cash flow, especially in the early stages.

Gauging potential demand is vital. Conduct surveys or focus groups to gather feedback and create minimum viable products (MVPs) for practical market testing. This approach minimizes initial investment and allows for iterative development based on real user needs.

Seek mentorship from experienced entrepreneurs and consult with professionals like financial advisors, attorneys, or business consultants for expert guidance.

Remember, this is an iterative process. Be prepared to refine your business idea based on feedback and market shifts. By applying these strategies and embracing continuous adaptation, you can turn your entrepreneurial dreams into a thriving reality during retirement.

> ### Guiding Tip: Calculated Courage
>
> Entrepreneurship in retirement isn't about taking wild risks but about making calculated decisions. Understanding the landscape, knowing your financial limits, and preparing for challenges can turn risks into well-thought-out ventures with high reward potential.

Balancing Risks and Rewards in Entrepreneurship

Venturing into the realm of entrepreneurship requires a balanced understanding of the potential rewards and the risks involved. Embracing this exciting path offers the possibility of personal fulfillment and the thrill of bringing new ideas to life. However, it's important to recognize that starting a business carries inherent risks. The market environment is constantly evolving, presenting challenges that can be particularly daunting for those just entering the business world.

Moreover, the commitment entrepreneurship demands can impact the work-life balance you've established in your retirement years. While it's true that many new businesses face significant hurdles, this shouldn't discourage you. Instead, consider it a call to proceed with both caution and optimism.

Guiding Tip: Why New Businesses Fail, and Warning Signs

1. Lack of Funding or Poor Financial Management:
Warning Signs: Running out of cash quickly, difficulty securing loans, inconsistent budgeting, failing to track expenses.

2. Inadequate Market Research & Misunderstanding Your Customer:
Warning Signs: Poor sales figures, high customer churn (customers not returning), negative customer feedback, difficulty reaching your target audience.

3. Flawed Business Model or Unsustainable Competitive Advantage:
Warning Signs: Difficulty competing on price or features, failing to differentiate your product/service, lack of innovation, limited market opportunity.

4. Ineffective Marketing and Sales Strategies:
Warning Signs: Low brand awareness, inability to generate leads, difficulty closing sales, high customer acquisition cost.

CONTINUED ON NEXT PAGE...

> ## Guiding Tip: Why New Businesses Fail, and Warning Signs
>
> ...CONTINUED FROM PREVIOUS PAGE
>
> **5. Poor Management and Leadership:**
> Warning Signs: High employee turnover, lack of clear direction or goals, operational inefficiencies, internal conflicts.
>
> **6. External Factors:**
> Warning Signs: Economic downturns, unexpected legal or regulatory changes, disruptions in the supply chain, natural disasters.

The good news: Proactive strategies can help mitigate the risks. A well-crafted business plan, outlining goals, strategies, and risk management tactics, serves as your roadmap. Financial preparedness is crucial, ensuring a safety net for both personal and business needs during the initial growth stage. Furthermore, continuous learning equips you to adapt to the ever-evolving market.

The potential rewards are equally significant. Entrepreneurship allows you to rekindle dormant passions and pursue long-held interests, leading to deep personal fulfillment. Financial success can not only generate additional income but also create a lasting legacy for future generations. The journey itself expands your network, fostering new connections and enriching your life.

Financial Planning for Entrepreneurial Ventures

Embarking on an entrepreneurial venture in retirement is an exhilarating way to channel years of experience into a fulfilling project. However, it requires careful financial planning to support the venture's success without jeopardizing your financial security. Here's how you can navigate the financial planning essential for supporting your business dreams.

The allocation of financial resources towards a new business must be done with careful consideration of your overall retirement plan. It's crucial to assess your financial landscape, determining how much of your retirement savings can be safely invested in a new venture without compromising your lifestyle. Diversifying income sources, such as combining pension income, savings, and potential business revenue, can mitigate risks associated with entrepreneurship.

Creating a detailed budget for your business is foundational. This budget should account for startup costs—such as equipment, marketing, and any necessary licenses or permits—as well as ongoing expenses like utilities, inventory, and insurance. It's also wise to allocate a contingency fund within this budget to cover unforeseen costs, ensuring your venture can weather the unpredictable nature of business operations.

> **Guiding Tip: Watch Cash Flow**
>
> Project cash flow in detail. It is common for a new business to be making a healthy profit on paper, but not have cash for expenses. It is largely a case of getting the timing right for income and receipts. If necessary, design packages to encourage early payments and follow up on collections.

Keeping startup costs in check involves researching and identifying the most cost-effective solutions for your business needs. For ongoing expenses, regular review and adjustment of your budget based on actual business performance can help maintain financial health. Tools such as accounting software can simplify tracking expenses and revenue, providing clear insights into your business's financial status.

Consulting with a financial advisor who has experience in entrepreneurial finance can be invaluable. They can offer guidance tailored to your unique situation, helping you to structure your financial planning in a way that supports both your business goals and your retirement security.

Entrepreneurship, especially in retirement, should also allow for a healthy work-life balance. This balance means not allowing the financial aspects of running your business to overshadow the personal fulfillment it brings. Setting clear boundaries for work hours and budgeting for personal leisure and relaxation can contribute to overall well-being. Remember, the goal of starting a business in retirement often extends beyond financial gain to include personal satisfaction and a sense of purpose.

Financial planning for an entrepreneurial venture also involves preparing for the long-term sustainability of both the business and your retirement lifestyle. This preparation might include exploring insurance options to protect the business and personal assets, investigating ways to reinvest profits for growth, and planning for eventual business succession or sale.

> ### Guiding Tip: Smart Budgeting for Success
>
> Effectively managing your financial resources lays the foundation for a successful entrepreneurial journey in retirement. It's about more than numbers on a spreadsheet; it's about strategically allocating your assets to fuel your business while safeguarding your retirement.

Embracing Innovation

In this section, I'll cover two essential elements that can significantly impact the success of your venture: innovation and adaptability.

Innovation drives entrepreneurship by fostering creative thinking, unique problem-solving, and fresh perspectives. It breathes new life into business endeavors, ensuring relevance and competitiveness. As a second act entrepreneur, you can leverage your lifetime of experience and expertise in innovative ways, applying your knowledge to create market value and succeed in a rapidly changing world.

In a crowded marketplace, innovative ideas and approaches can set your business apart. Retirees can use their unique backgrounds and perspectives to identify niche opportunities and develop creative solutions that resonate with their target audience. The big hit is disruption; when you create a new way of doing something or unique products or product modification that rock the business sector.

Change is inevitable, but how you respond to it can make all the difference. You must cultivate a mindset of adaptability, embracing change as an opportunity for growth rather than a threat. Being open to new strategies, technologies, and business models is crucial.

In the entrepreneurial world, setbacks and failures are part of the journey. Adaptability involves learning from these experiences and adjusting your approach accordingly. It's about resilience and the willingness to pivot when necessary.

Tips for Fostering Creativity

Stay curious: Curiosity is the fuel for creativity. Keep asking questions, exploring new ideas, and seeking inspiration from various sources. Retirees have the advantage of time and life experience to feed their curiosity.

Collaborate and network: Surround yourself with a diverse

network of individuals who can bring fresh perspectives to the table. Collaboration can spark innovative ideas and lead to valuable partnerships.

Embrace continuous learning to stay current with industry trends and new technologies. Keeping your skills up-to-date not only maintains your relevance but also positions you to adapt effectively to changing market dynamics.

Cultivate a growth mindset that sees challenges as opportunities to learn and improve. Be open to feedback and be willing to iterate on your ideas.

Don't be afraid to experiment with new approaches in your business. Test different strategies and gather data to inform your decisions. Entrepreneurship in retirement allows you the flexibility to try, fail, and try again.

Seek inspiration. Explore other successful entrepreneurs' journeys and stories. Learn from their experiences and adapt their strategies to your unique situation.

Innovation and adaptability are the twin engines that can propel you to success in your entrepreneurial endeavors during retirement. By embracing innovation, you can leverage your knowledge and experience to create fresh, valuable solutions. Simultaneously, adaptability ensures that you remain resilient in the face of changing market dynamics.

With a curious mindset, a willingness to collaborate, and a commitment to continuous learning, you can foster creativity and stay open to new ideas. Embracing change and viewing challenges as opportunities for growth will enable you to thrive as an entrepreneur in retirement, creating a fulfilling second act filled with innovation and adaptability.

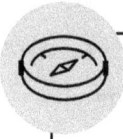

> ### Guiding Tip: Adaptability - Your Business's Superpower
>
> In a world where market dynamics shift rapidly, adaptability is crucial. It's about being prepared to pivot, whether in response to technological advancements, consumer trends, or unexpected challenges. Fostering a culture of creativity and openness to change is key to entrepreneurial resilience and success.

Practical Steps to Launching an Entrepreneurial Venture

If you are contemplating entrepreneurship as your second act, converting a vision into a viable business requires methodical planning and execution. Here is a step-by-step guide to embarking on this exhilarating journey.

Idea validation: Begin by validating your business idea through market research. Identify your target audience, assess competitors, and confirm there's a demand for your product or service.

Business planning: Develop a comprehensive business

plan that outlines your business model, marketing strategy, financial projections, operational logistics, and risk analysis. This document will be crucial for guiding your venture and securing funding.

Securing funding: Explore various funding options, including personal savings, small business loans, or investments from family and friends. Crowdfunding platforms may also offer a viable avenue for raising capital.

Building your brand: Create a strong brand identity that resonates with your target market. This includes developing a business name, logo, and a marketing strategy to build brand awareness.

Launching your business: With planning and funding in place, take the plunge and launch your business. Focus on building a solid customer base and gather feedback to refine your offerings.

Seeking mentorship: Connect with other entrepreneurs and seek mentorship. Experienced business owners can provide invaluable advice, support, and networking opportunities.

I highly recommend reading "Lean Marketing" by Allan Dib; it's one of the most insightful and practical business books I've ever encountered. The strategies and principles outlined in this book can transform your approach to marketing and help enhance your business success.

> **Guiding Tip: Are You Ready to Jump?**
>
> Taking the leap into entrepreneurship is both challenging and rewarding. By following these practical steps, retirees can navigate the journey with confidence, working toward turning their business dreams into reality.

Fostering Personal Growth Through Entrepreneurship

Navigating the ups and downs of entrepreneurship teaches valuable lessons in adaptability and resilience. Learning to pivot in response to market feedback, financial challenges, or other obstacles is a testament to the dynamic nature of personal growth through entrepreneurship.

Embarking on an entrepreneurial venture in retirement isn't just about starting a business—it's a journey of personal growth and development. Through the challenges and successes of entrepreneurship, retirees can discover new strengths, develop new skills, and experience profound personal change. Entrepreneurship demands a broad skill set, from financial management to marketing.

You can use this opportunity to learn new skills or refine existing ones, to learn how to pivot in response to market feedback, financial challenges, or other obstacles. Overcoming the hurdles of starting and running a business can significantly boost self-confidence. Each small victory reinforces the belief in one's abilities, encouraging further exploration and innovation.

> ### Guiding Tip: An Amazing Opportunity
> Entrepreneurship as a second act is more than a path to financial independence; it's a catalyst for personal growth. It challenges you to adapt and thrive, proving that personal development knows no age limit.

Shine First Today: Starting a Passion Project Before Retirement

Now is a perfect time to embark on a passion project, something that resonates deeply with your interests and aspirations. Starting now can provide immense fulfillment and a sense of purpose, enriching your life both today and in the future. Consider turning your passions into a meaningful venture that not only brings joy but also adds value to others' lives.

A few years ago, I faced crippling panic attacks and anxiety. To overcome these challenges, I decided to write a book on the subject. Although the book isn't published yet, this endeavor led me to start the Shine First Today podcast. Sharing my journey and insights with others has been incredibly rewarding, and it has opened new doors for me to connect with and inspire people facing similar struggles.

Moreover, this journey also inspired me to write and publish a goal-setting planner called "Thriving in the Fast Lane: 90 Days to Set, Plan, and Achieve Your Goals." For more information, check out: www.ShineFirstToday.com

This project has not only helped others achieve their goals but has also provided me with a profound sense of accomplishment and purpose. Starting a passion project can have similar effects for you, providing a fulfilling way to utilize your skills and experiences in a new, exciting context.

Starting now, before retirement, allows you to build a foundation and gain momentum. It can be a gradual transition from your current career, providing a smooth shift into your post-retirement life. You don't have to wait until you retire to begin; instead, use this time to explore your interests and start something that excites you.

By embarking on a passion project now, you create opportunities for continuous growth and learning. It's a powerful way to leverage your experience and knowledge, transforming them into something new and valuable. Whether it's writing, like me, or any other pursuit that ignites your passion, starting now can lead to a fulfilling and enriching retirement journey.

Closing Thoughts: Embark on Your Entrepreneurial Journey

In this brief journey, we've explored the exciting prospect of entrepreneurship as a second act in retirement. While space constraints have limited us to outlining the basics, consider this discussion a foundational framework—a starting point from which to expand your understanding.

For deeper insights into the themes and strategies we've touched upon, I encourage you to visit the resource landing page at www.EarlyStartRetirement.com. There, you'll find comprehensive guidance, additional tools, and further reading on entrepreneurship.

As you contemplate starting a business in retirement, remember that the possibilities are vast, and the rewards can be deeply fulfilling. The resource page is designed to support you on this journey, offering valuable information and inspiration to help you navigate this new venture with confidence and clarity.

Should you decide to embark on this exciting path, I wholeheartedly wish you success and fulfillment. Your entrepreneurial journey can be a source of great joy and purpose, enriching both your retirement and the lives of those you touch.

CHAPTER THREE

Living Abroad: The International Retirement Experience

Retirement, a time often earmarked for slowing down, also offers an invigorating prospect of new beginnings. Imagine swapping the familiar rhythm of your local community for the vibrant beat of a bustling market in Thailand, the serene pace of a Portuguese coastal town, or the lively hum of a Latin American city. This chapter explores the idea of retiring abroad—a path less trodden, yet rich with potential for those daring to step beyond borders.

For many, the dream of international retirement conjures images of sun-soaked beaches, cultural immersion, and the freedom to explore the world at a leisurely pace. It's a vision where daily life is not just lived but savored, where every sunrise promises not just another day, but another adventure. But, as with any significant life change, the move from dream to reality is layered with considerations, from the logistical to the emotional.

In this exploration, we will traverse the landscapes of international retirement, examining the magnetic pull of distant shores and the practical steps to anchor your dreams in reality. We will meet retirees who have woven their lives into new cultures, learning from their successes and challenges. Each story, each piece of advice, is a beacon guiding you through your deliberations and decisions.

Retiring abroad is not merely a change of address—it's a renaissance of the self. It's an opportunity to redefine who you are in a global context, to reinvent yourself every day, and to discover latent passions that only emerge when you step out of your comfort zone. Whether it's through learning a new language, building friendships in a foreign land, or simply finding tranquility in a change of scenery, international retirement is a bold assertion of life's richness post-career.

As we unpack the layers of this exciting chapter in life, we invite you to reflect on the mosaic of opportunities and weigh them against the practicalities of such a choice. This chapter is both a map and a mirror—guiding you through the terrain of international retirement while asking you to look deeply at your aspirations and intentions.

The world is vast, and your spirit for adventure is a compass pointing towards the unknown. Let's journey together into the heart of what it means to retire not just away from something but toward a world of possibilities. Welcome to Chapter 3 - Living Abroad: The International Retirement Experience.

Weighing the Pros and Cons of an Overseas Retirement

Retiring abroad is an exhilarating notion, one teeming with images of pristine beaches, cultural escapades, and the fresh start many yearn for as they close one chapter and begin another. Yet, the leap into a life overseas is both an art and a science – a balance of emotional desires and rational considerations.

The siren call of an overseas retirement beckons with a bouquet of benefits. Financial incentives often top the list, as many expatriates find the cost of living significantly lower than in the United States. In places like Costa Rica, Portugal, or Malaysia, your dollar stretches further, subsidizing a lifestyle lush with leisure and luxury that might be untenable stateside on a fixed income.

But there's a richness to this choice that transcends fiscal savings. Immersing oneself in a new culture brings an invigorating freshness to life. Days become canvases for language lessons, cooking classes, and historical exploration. It's not uncommon for retirees to discover new hobbies or rekindle old passions now that time is a friend, not a foe.

Healthcare, an acute concern for many retirees, can also be a point of attraction. Numerous countries touted for their retiree-friendly environments boast healthcare systems that rival—and occasionally outperform—those in the U.S., often at a fraction of the cost. This access to affordable, quality healthcare provides peace of mind and the freedom to enjoy this new life chapter.

The social fabric of expatriate communities is another draw. The camaraderie found in these circles is instantaneous and strong, forged in the shared experience of adventure and adaptation. Bonds are quickly formed, often resulting in a supportive network that feels like family.

But every rose has its thorns, and retiring abroad is no bed of petals. The cons, while navigable, are worth pondering with the same enthusiasm one gives the pros.

Language barriers may be the first hurdle, potentially isolating those who do not venture out or struggle to learn the local tongue. The nuances of daily life—negotiating a lease, going to the doctor, even grocery shopping—can be frustrating exercises in miscommunication.

Cultural differences run deeper than the initial shock of unfamiliar customs or etiquette; they can impact your very integration into the community. Long-standing traditions may seem charming at first glance but can feel exclusionary to an outsider trying to find their place in a new society.

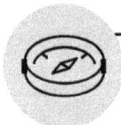

Guiding Tip: The Top Retirement Destination in Asia for Americans

If you're thinking about retiring in Southeast Asia, the Philippines should be a top contender.

CONTINUED ON NEXT PAGE...

Guiding Tip: The Top Retirement Destination in Asia for Americans

...CONTINUED FROM PREVIOUS PAGE

This tropical archipelago of over 7,000 islands offers a unique blend of cultures, stunning natural beauty, and a warm and welcoming atmosphere. The Philippines was a former US territory, and its culture is still influenced by American trends. English is widely spoken and is the official language of education, business, and international relations. You'll also find traces of the country's Spanish colonial past, evident in its architecture, cuisine, and language.

There are more than 400,000 Americans living and working in the Philippines, including many active and retired US service personnel. This large expat community creates a supportive and familiar environment for Americans settling in the country.

The Philippines offers several different retirement visas including one open to foreign nationals aged 50 and above who are retired from the armed forces of the US or other countries with military ties or agreements with the Philippine government.

Navigating the legal aspects of visas, residency requirements, and tax obligations can be challenging and complex. These issues, if not handled correctly from the start, can pose significant hurdles and dampen the initial excitement of moving abroad.

Healthcare, while often affordable, may vary in quality and accessibility, particularly in remote or less developed areas. It's crucial to understand these differences and plan accordingly, as they can significantly impact your wellbeing.

Being far from family and friends is another important consideration. While technology helps bridge the gap, physical distance and time zones can strain relationships and lead to missed milestones.

Weighing the pros and cons of international retirement involves balancing practicalities with possibilities. It's about embracing the unknown while preparing meticulously and measuring the tangible benefits against the intangibles. As you consider a new life in places like Spain or Vietnam, assess all aspects to truly gauge your readiness for this grand adventure.

Choosing Your Corner of the World

Embarking on an overseas retirement requires choosing a destination as much with your head as with your heart. This decision, potentially lasting just 3 to 5 years, invites not just careful consideration but also a bit of dreaming. Let's explore how to select that perfect corner of the world that aligns not only with your budget but also with your aspirations.

To start, envision the daily backdrop of your life. Do rolling vineyards stir your spirit, or are you more captivated by the rhythmic lapping of ocean waves? The climate is a palpable factor in your comfort and happiness, and retiring abroad offers a buffet of choices—from the eternal spring of the Ecuadorian highlands to the crisp, autumnal air of a Tuscan village.

The cost of living is a critical compass in charting your course. It's essential to align your retirement dreams with your financial reality. Fortunately, in many sought-after expat havens, a modest retirement income stream can fund a lifestyle that's rich with cultural experiences and local delights. By comparing living costs—housing, utilities, food, transportation—you can prioritize what matters most, whether it's gourmet dining, travel, or simply the serenity of a comfortable home.

Healthcare quality, accessibility, and affordability must be at the forefront of any retiree's mind. In assessing a potential new home, scrutinize the healthcare system. Is quality care readily available? How do the costs compare to those at home, and what insurance will you need? Many countries that attract retirees, like Mexico or Thailand, offer excellent healthcare at a fraction of U.S. prices, but it's important to conduct thorough research to ensure your health won't be compromised.

Next, ponder the cultural variants of your potential new home. Cultural compatibility is the undercurrent of daily joy in retirement.

Language is another facet of cultural compatibility. While it's possible to live comfortably without mastering a new language, learning the local tongue opens doors to deeper relationships and enriches your experience. Consider destinations where the language inspires you or where language services are available to support your learning journey.

The legalities of establishing residency cannot be overlooked. Some countries roll out the welcome mat with retiree-specific visas that offer perks and ease the transition. Others present a labyrinth of bureaucracy that can challenge even the most patient soul. Research and perhaps consult with a legal expert to understand the residency process for your country of choice.

Don't forget about connectivity to home. If frequent visits from family or the option to return stateside easily are important, consider proximity to international airports and direct flights.

In rounding out your choice, it's helpful to hear the stories of those who've already made the leap. Connect with expat communities, both online and in person, to glean insights into the realities of life in your chosen destination. There's no substitute for the wisdom of those who are living your dream.

Choosing your corner of the world for retirement is not a one-size-fits-all decision. It is a beautiful blend of practicality and aspiration, a balance of what is needed to live comfortably and what is desired to live joyfully. Take the time to let your heart wander, let your mind calculate, and find that sweet spot where your heart sings —you've found your home.

Legalities and Logistics for Your International Retirement

Beyond the excitement of international retirement, you

need to address the legalities and logistics that support your dream life abroad.

Start by navigating each country's unique legal requirements. Securing a visa is essential, with many countries offering specific retiree visas that may include benefits like tax breaks but also require proof of consistent income and health insurance.

Income documentation is crucial. You'll need to provide pension statements, social security documentation, or proof of investments to meet the country's financial thresholds for residency.

Taxes are another key consideration. Understand the tax treaties between your home country and your new one, which will affect money transfers, pension access, and savings. Some countries offer tax-free foreign income, while others have more complex tax structures.

Addressing these legal and logistical elements ensures a smooth transition to your international retirement.

Healthcare logistics are crucial. Research whether you need private health insurance or can use the local healthcare system. Understand coverage, out-of-pocket costs, and how your visa status affects eligibility.

Guiding Tip: Start as a Digital Nomad

Governments in many countries are issuing 6- or 12-month visas to remote workers (digital nomads). This might be a good way to begin a migration if it fits your skill set. See Chapter 5.

Property laws add another layer of complexity. Some countries restrict foreign ownership or require a specific visa. Consult a local attorney to understand property ownership nuances, including taxes, inheritance laws, and potential issues with repatriating funds after selling property.

Consider your pension and social security. Determine if you can receive these benefits abroad, potential currency exchange fees, and any penalties for living overseas. Some countries have agreements for seamless benefit transfers, while others require navigating complex bureaucracy.

Addressing these legal and logistical aspects is vital for a smooth transition to your overseas retirement. Each decision is a piece of the puzzle, creating a comprehensive picture of your new life abroad. While it requires diligence and expert guidance, the reward is a retirement crafted on your terms.

Cultural Considerations: Integrating and Thriving Abroad

Retirement abroad is more than a change of scenery; it's an opportunity for personal growth through new cultural experiences. To weave into the fabric of a foreign culture requires curiosity, respect, and an open heart and mind. This challenge of integration can turn into a rewarding, multifaceted retirement.

Language is a key to unlocking conversations, friendships, and local secrets. Basic proficiency can open doors and show your willingness to adapt. Taking language classes, either before you move or once you're there, and using technology like apps and online platforms for flexible learning paths, can help build these essential bridges.

Cultural integration goes beyond language. It's about understanding and respecting customs and traditions, participating in local festivals, adopting new food habits, and learning social etiquette. Volunteering can also help you connect with locals and give back to your new community. Balancing new cultural experiences with your own traditions creates a fulfilling and enriching retirement, turning challenges into opportunities for deeper connections and unexpected joys.

Guiding Tip: Be Prepared for Culture Shock and Being Homesick

Moving to a new country is exciting. There is generally a honeymoon period when everything is new, noteworthy, and rosy. After some time, maybe several months or more, some aspects of living abroad (such as dealing with bureaucracy, corruption, the absence of selected home comforts, etc.) and a measure of homesickness, might conspire to make moving to your new location seem like a bad idea. When this happens, and it's more likely to be when rather than if, I urge you to ride it out.

CONTINUED ON NEXT PAGE...

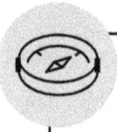

> ### Guiding Tip: Be Prepared for Culture Shock and Being Homesick
> ...CONTINUED FROM PREVIOUS PAGE
>
> Try to minimize your interactions with the negative issues and focus on the good things. The feeling might repeat from time to time with declining impact. After you have handled one of these bouts, you will likely return to loving your new home again.

Countdown to Departure: A Pre-Move Roadmap

As the countdown to your international move begins, crafting a roadmap is crucial for a smooth departure. This pre-move guide, tailored for those ready to embrace retirement across borders, provides some practical steps. Be sure to adjust the timeline and actions to your own circumstances.

Time of Departure (T) -6 Months: Research and Documentation

Begin with research. Explore comprehensive guides about your chosen destination, focusing on expatriate experiences and local customs. This is the time to become familiar with the subtleties of your future home from afar.

Simultaneously, begin gathering important documents. Ensure your passport has ample validity—many countries require it to be valid for at least six months beyond your date of arrival. It may not be required initially but you could well find it useful in the future if you have copies of your birth certificate, marriage certificate, education and professional certifications, etc. Begin the application or renewal processes for visas, residency permits, and other necessary legal documentation. Be sure to check if any documents require apostilles or official translations.

Check with the authorities at your destination and your physician to determine if any specific vaccinations are required (they may have differing recommendations). If you take maintenance medication, prepare to pack a sufficient supply and bring a letter from your doctor to assist in obtaining refills.

This is also a good time to consider your housing situation. If you own your home, decide whether to sell, rent, or leave it in the care of a trusted friend or family member. If you plan to rent out your house, you should appoint someone local to interface with the tenant. If you are currently renting, be sure to check the terms of lease to ensure a hassle-free departure.

Start planning your initial accommodation in your destination—whether it's renting a property or booking a hotel or temporary housing until you find/complete occupancy of your new permanent residence.

> ## Guiding Tip: Think Carefully Before Cutting Ties
>
> Some expats bemoan severing ties with their home country too soon. In particular, some who sold their real estate when moving abroad later regret it, finding themselves priced out of the housing market in their home country due to rising property prices.

T-4 Months: Health and Home Affairs

Four months out, address health concerns. Schedule medical, dental, and vision check-ups, and complete any outstanding procedures. Investigate your healthcare options abroad, including international health insurance that covers you in your new country, and perhaps includes emergency airlift to medical facilities if you are moving off grid. Securing this early avoids the pitfalls of uncovered medical expenses.

T-3 Months: Financial Foresight

With three months to go, scrutinize your financial landscape. Notify your bank of your move to maintain access to your accounts and reduce the risk of fraud alerts when accessing funds overseas.

Consider setting up an account with a bank in your new country, preferably a US international bank with global branches. Check that anti-money laundering laws won't delay or hinder international transfers.

Familiarize yourself with the fastest and most cost-effective ways to transfer funds. Different services may offer better efficiency than conventional banking. Ensure the companies you choose are reliable and trustworthy. Investigate tax obligations in both your home country and abroad to avoid legal complications.

For more detailed information and resources, visit our resource page at www.EarlyStartRetirement.com. Consulting an international tax advisor can also help navigate the complexities of dual taxation agreements.

T-1 Month: The Logistics of Living

As the departure progresses, tackle the logistics of the move. If you're taking belongings with you, decide what to pack, what to store, and what to discard. Contact international movers and obtain quotes, shipping timelines, and advice.

A friend of mine, moving to the Middle East, discovered on arrival that his books were temporarily confiscated and subject to censorship. He also found that his local contact was able to work some magic to avoid having certain pages removed from the Encyclopedia Brittanica.

T-2 Weeks: Farewells and Finalities

In the last two weeks, say your goodbyes. Host a farewell gathering or visit your favorite local spots to bid adieu. Emotionally, these moments are precious, as they provide closure and celebrate the beginning of your new adventure. Double-check your travel arrangements—flights, airport transfers, and accommodations upon arrival. Ensure you have local currency and understand the exchange rate.

T-1 Week: The Final Countdown

In the final week, confirm everything is in order. Check in with your international mover, review travel insurance, and verify that all necessary documents are accessible and copied.

On a personal note, pack a carry-on with essentials for your first few days abroad. Include important documents, medications, a change of clothes, and any personal items that will make your new space feel like home.

In the stillness before the journey, reflect on the significance of the step you're about to take. Retirement abroad is not merely a relocation; it's a renaissance of self, a promise of new beginnings. With each task completed on this pre-move roadmap, you weave another strand of assurance into the fabric of your future, ensuring that your transition to a life abroad is as seamless as the fusion of old memories and new horizons.

Keeping Your Roots: Staying Connected Across the Globe

Though oceans may lie between, maintaining this connection sustains relationships, nourishes roots, and ensures that 'home' is never out of reach, no matter where you roam. This section offers heartfelt advice on nurturing these vital connections from afar.

Embrace Technology: Your Digital Bridge

In today's digital age, technology is the gossamer thread that binds us, irrespective of distance. Equip yourself with a reliable laptop, tablet, or smartphone—tools that are your gateway to instant communication. Learn to use video calling platforms such as Google Meet, Zoom, FaceTime, etc.; these services shrink miles into pixels, allowing face-to-face interaction with loved ones at the click of a button. Other social media platforms like WhatsApp, Messenger, Viber, etc. which also have written chat also help you stay abreast of happenings in your friends' and family's lives, contributing to a sense of daily presence and inclusion.

Time Zone Tango: Schedule Regular Calls

When you retire abroad, time zones can tangle your attempts to connect. To avoid this, establish a regular schedule for calls and virtual visits. Whether it's a Sunday Skype brunch or a Wednesday WhatsApp catch-up, having these fixtures gives you and your loved ones a reliable window to commune, laugh, and share stories.

Snail Mail and Care Packages: The Joy of Tangibles

Despite the speed and convenience of digital communication, there is an undeniable charm in the tangibility of snail mail. Send postcards, letters, or care packages—physical tokens of love that can be touched and treasured. Receiving a handwritten note or a parcel filled with local trinkets and treats can bridge emotional distances and provide a tangible presence in each other's lives.

Local Numbers: A Call Away

Consider obtaining a virtual local phone number in the U.S. so that family and friends who are not social media savvy reach you easily.

Virtual Celebrations: Shared Memories from Afar

Birthdays, anniversaries, and holidays need not be solitary affairs. With a bit of creativity, you can be part of the festivities. Plan virtual parties, coordinate meal deliveries across continents, and watch the grandkids' recital or baseball game via social media. These shared experiences continue to weave the fabric of family life, no matter the miles.

Community Involvement: New Experiences for Old Friends

As you assimilate into your new community abroad, involve your friends and family back home in your discoveries and experiences. Start a blog, a vlog, or an email newsletter chronicling your adventures. Invite them to visit and experience your new world firsthand. This not only keeps the connection alive but also enriches it with new dimensions and shared experiences.

Nurturing New and Old Friendships

Remember to cultivate new friendships in your new locale,

because they can provide support and companionship on-site. Meanwhile, encourage your friends from home to remain an active part of your life. Mutual efforts in maintaining these relationships signify their importance and can make the physical distance feel insignificant.

The Home Base: Periodic Returns

Plan periodic visits back to your homeland, if possible. These returns serve as a refreshing dip into the waters of familiarity and provide an opportunity to recharge amidst the comforts of home, surrounded by the embrace of long-term friendships and family bonds.

Despite the distances of an international retirement, staying connected to your roots is a must. It requires effort, intention, and a sprinkle of creativity, but the emotional rewards are vast, ensuring that retirees can have the best of both worlds—a new life filled with adventure and exploration without losing the cherished connections that define who they are and where they've come from.

Global Pioneers: Success Stories from Abroad

In the journey of life, retirement abroad is akin to the unfolding of a second act on the world stage, ripe with the possibility of personal reinvention. The narratives of retirees who have boldly crafted a life beyond their native shores stand as testaments to the fulfillment such a choice can bring. Their stories, varied as the destinations they've chosen, offer inspiration, guidance, and the affirmation that retiring abroad can indeed be a rich experience. Let's review a collection of success stories that encapsulate the joys and triumphs of becoming a global pioneer in retirement.

Embracing La Dolce Vita: The Harrisons in Italy

The Harrisons always dreamed of a retirement drenched in culture and history. They found their haven in the rolling hills of Tuscany, where they now host cooking and art classes. Merging their love for Italian cuisine with a desire to connect with others, they've become fixtures in their local community, embracing 'la dolce vita' while sharing their journey with fellow expats through a vibrant blog that's peppered with tales of vineyard tours and truffle hunts.

A New Chapter in the Land of the Rising Sun: Karen's Solo Adventure

When Karen's nest emptied, she packed her bags for Japan, a place that had long captivated her imagination. She had already taken language classes. Armed with a love for the language and a zeal for teaching, she now spends her days as an English tutor, weaving herself into the fabric of her neighborhood in Kyoto. Her story highlights the empowering nature of solo travel and the deep satisfaction that comes from continuous learning and cultural immersion.

Philanthropic Ventures in South America: The

Chen Legacy

Michael and Li Chen's retirement is driven by a mission to give back. Settling in Ecuador, they've founded a small non-profit to support local artisans. Their efforts have not only brought economic vitality to the community but also created a cross-cultural exchange that enriches both the local residents and the expats who volunteer with them. Their journey illustrates how retirement can be a launching pad for impactful philanthropic work.

The Art of Adaptation: The Gomez Family in Portugal

Retiring to Portugal, the Gomez family discovered the delicate art of adaptation. They weave their Hispanic heritage into their newfound Portuguese lifestyle, creating a beautiful blend that resonates within their seaside town. Their warm household has become a melting pot of cultures, celebrated through music-filled gatherings that echo with both fado and flamenco, illustrating the harmony that can be achieved through cultural fusion.

Culinary Crossroads: Chef Jackson's French Farewell

Chef Jackson bid adieu her American bistro to fulfill a dream of baking beneath the French skies. In a quaint patisserie in Bordeaux, her pastries have won over the hearts (and palates) of locals, and her apprenticeship programs have attracted budding bakers from around the globe. Her story is a testament to the universal language of food and the opportunities to share one's passion in a foreign land.

Each of these pioneers, with their diverse backgrounds and aspirations, demonstrates that there's no singular way to retire abroad; there is a multitude of paths one can take, each offering its own unique rewards. They show that with determination, openness, and a bit of courage, retirement can be not just a period of relaxation, but a chapter filled with growth, contribution, and a global web of experiences.

Their lives underscore the most poignant lesson for those contemplating a retirement overseas: that the pursuit of a dream, the willingness to step out of one's comfort zone, and the embrace of new cultures can lead to a retirement that's as fulfilling as it is adventurous. These global pioneers set the course, lighting the way for future retirees to follow in their footsteps into a world where retirement is not an end but a vibrant new beginning.

A Healthy Horizon: Managing Your Health Overseas

Maintaining health is crucial in retirement, especially abroad. Proactive planning is essential, research healthcare systems and secure reliable insurance. For example, the Harrisons' move to Tuscany included arranging private insurance to complement Italy's public services, providing peace of mind.

Navigating local healthcare systems is vital. Learning the language, as Karen did in Japan, can enhance communication with healthcare professionals. Building community ties, like the Chens in Ecuador, provides valuable local healthcare recommendations. Embrace local remedies and stay informed on health policies to ensure robust health plans.

New Horizons: Cultivating a Life of Adventure

Retirement abroad is an adventure filled with new experiences. It's not just a change of scenery, but a profound shift in lifestyle, offering personal growth and cultural immersion. Imagine learning new languages and exploring historical sites, turning everyday interactions into meaningful connections.

While adventure comes with challenges, overcoming them builds resilience. Craft your retirement adventure with care, choosing a path that resonates with your deepest yearnings. The true essence of adventure lies in embracing change and exploring life's limitless potential.

The Long View: Expect the Unexpected

Retirement abroad promises new cultures and cost-effective living but comes with uncertainties. Proactive planning and flexible strategies are essential. Have insurance for health, repatriation, and property, and maintain a financial buffer for unexpected expenses.

Legal literacy is crucial. Understand visa regulations and property laws, and consider maintaining a home base for security. Cultivate resilience and resourcefulness to handle challenges abroad, ensuring a smooth and fulfilling retirement.

Embracing International Living While Still Working

Consider starting your international adventure before retirement. Technology allows for flexible work arrangements, making it possible to live abroad while working. Whether taking a gap year or becoming a digital nomad, plan financially and understand tax implications to blend work and international living seamlessly.

Planning a gap year involves saving funds and budgeting for unexpected expenses. Digital nomads should ensure reliable internet access and use cloud-based solutions. Understanding tax regulations and professional requirements in both home and host countries is crucial for a smooth transition.

· ▶

Key Takeaways

Imagine what life would be like if you pursued retirement abroad. By adopting a mindset of strategic optimism, you can plan for the unexpected to ensure your overseas adventure remains fulfilling and joyful. Envision savoring the excitement of new experiences while maintaining a sense of security and tranquility.

- Plan Strategically: Prepare for unexpected events to ensure a fulfilling and joyful overseas retirement.
- Expand Your Life: Retiring abroad is more than a change in location; it's an opportunity to expand your experiences and perspectives.
- Understand Practicalities: Consider visas, healthcare, and cultural adaptation. Learn from the stories of other retirees who have navigated similar paths.
- Take the First Step: Start planning your global retirement by envisioning your ideal life abroad. Create a vision board or hold a brainstorming session to gather all your ideas in one place.
- Prepare and Adapt: Learn how to prepare, adapt, and thrive in your new environment. The world is your canvas, filled with opportunities for culture, community, and personal growth.
- I love a Vision Board: If you plan to live overseas for 3-5 years, start with a vision board or brainstorming session to gather all your ideas. Consider what you want from this experience and how you can achieve it. The horizon calls, the adventure beckons—how will you answer?

Step forward into the world with an open heart and mind, eager for the lessons and luxuries that an international retirement can provide. The world awaits your unique imprint.

CHAPTER FOUR

Portfolio Lifestyle: Crafting a Portfolio of Passions

L et's depart from traditional views of retirement and embrace this phase of your life as a vibrant ascent into a world rich with possibilities and choices.

Gone are the days when retirement followed a singular, linear path. Today, it unfolds as a dynamic "portfolio lifestyle," where diversifying activities becomes the heartbeat of daily existence. This lifestyle empowers you to blend passions, interests, and dreams into a personalized portrait that celebrates your individuality and zest for life.

In this chapter, we will explore how you can craft a retirement that's as dynamic and multifaceted as you are. From reigniting past passions to discovering new interests, from embracing the excitement of travel to indulging in the joys of learning, and from finding purpose in volunteer work to possibly embarking on encore careers—the possibilities are endless.

We will also consider practical aspects such as balancing

these activities, managing time effectively, and ensuring financial sustainability to support your diverse pursuits. Real-life stories and examples will serve as both inspiration and a guide, helping you visualize what your unique portfolio lifestyle could look like.

Welcome to the journey of creating your diverse, fulfilling retirement, as you craft a portfolio of passions to enrich your life today and beyond.

Introduction to Portfolio Living: Your Multifaceted Retirement

Imagine retirement as a gallery of experiences, where each activity you choose hangs like a unique piece of art on the walls of your daily life. This is the heart of portfolio living, a strategic approach to retirement that weaves together a rich collection of activities to create a fulfilling mix for everyday existence. It's about diversifying your "life investments" to include not just financial stability but also personal growth, community involvement, and the pursuit of passion projects that ignite your spirit.

The concept of portfolio living stems from the financial world, where a diverse portfolio aims to spread risk and increase the chance of reward. Similarly, a diversified retirement lifestyle spreads the richness of experience across various aspects of life, increasing the overall quality of life and satisfaction.

Guiding Tip: Craft a Portfolio of Passions

The term "portfolio" isn't just for finances. Applying it to your retirement lifestyle encourages a diverse investment in activities that fulfill different parts of your life, much like a well-rounded investment portfolio.

The Early Start Retirement Plan recognizes that the definition of retirement is evolving. No longer does it only mean the cessation of work; it's now about choosing your engagements with the freedom that comes from financial planning and the wisdom of years. It's about selecting activities that offer enrichment and joy, challenge you, or provide comfort.

By viewing retirement through the lens of a portfolio lifestyle, you can craft a dynamic and fulfilling life. This approach allows you to blend passions, interests, and dreams into a personalized plan that celebrates your individuality and zest for life.

The rewards? They're numerous—enhanced mental acuity, better physical health, deeper social connections, and a more profound sense of purpose.

But how does one curate such a life? It starts with a reflection — an inventory of personal interests, values, and unexplored dreams. This process is not about filling time; it's about filling life with the activities that resonate most deeply. It requires a delicate balance, ensuring that each endeavor aligns with your energy levels, financial means, and overarching life goals.

Guiding Tip: One at a Time

Start by integrating one new activity at a time into your routine. This manageable approach helps prevent overwhelm and allows you to fully savor each new experience.

Cultivating Passions: Unearthing and Nurturing New Interests and Hobbies

With a portfolio lifestyle, cultivating your passions enhances your retirement years. It's also about unearthing and nurturing new interests and hobbies that may have lain dormant under the demands of a career and family life. This guide helps you rediscover your passions, turning "someday" dreams into "today's" pursuits, and infusing your daily life with joy and fulfillment as you embrace your passions now.

Exercise: Crafting Your Passion List

As we explored in Chapter 1, creating a "passion list" is a vibrant and enlightening exercise. Start by settling down with a cup of your favorite coffee or tea. Grab a large piece of blank paper and a pen or pencil, and let your imagination run free. Write down anything that ignites a spark of excitement or curiosity in you—this is your playground, so don't hold back!

Begin in the center of your paper and jot down a few things that interest you. Then, branch out from each idea, exploring what specifically excites you about each one. Allow your list to grow organically; you might find yourself with 50 or 60 intriguing ideas and subjects.

Now, think about how you can connect these interests. For example, if you're eager to travel and learn a new language, why not plan a trip to a country where that language is spoken? Or, if you want to learn painting and spend more time with your grandkids, consider enrolling in a painting workshop together. By weaving your interests together, you'll enhance your enjoyment and engagement in each activity.

Nurturing Your Interests

Once you've identified potential interests, the next step is to nurture them. This might mean taking classes—local community centers, libraries, and online platforms offer many options. Or it could involve joining clubs or groups where you can share these interests with others, which can be particularly fulfilling. Not only do you get to follow your passion, but you can also connect with like-minded individuals, fostering social connections that are vital in retirement.

Remember, the focus is on enjoyment and personal fulfillment, not on mastering or excelling in these activities. Give yourself the freedom to experiment and the permission to be a beginner. There's joy in the learning process itself, in the gradual unfolding of your abilities and understanding.

When I turned 50, I decided to treat myself to an art class at the local college. I took Drawing 101, and it absolutely changed my life. In addition to learning the basics of drawing, which has been fundamental as I've explored other interests like watercolor and oil painting, creating art is incredibly relaxing and restorative. It's almost like meditating in how effective it is at reducing stress, anxiety, and overwhelm. I didn't even know how to draw a stick figure, and now it's turned into a wonderful passion that I enjoy today and will continue to enjoy throughout my lifetime. This personal journey highlights the profound impact of nurturing new interests and how they can transform your retirement years into a time of joy and fulfillment.

Turning Passions into Purpose

Retirement isn't just a time to pursue hobbies; it's a wonderful opportunity to find a new sense of purpose through the things you love doing. For example, if you're a fan of knitting or sewing, why not craft cozy items for newborns in hospitals or create warm clothes for homeless shelters?

If you're a writer at heart, consider starting a blog to share your wealth of life experiences, or lend your pen to a local non-profit organization's newsletter. These aren't just activities to pass the time—they're ways to enrich both your life and the lives of others, providing a deep sense of purpose and accomplishment that makes retirement truly fulfilling.

As for me, I've always noticed a bit of yarn left over after my knitting projects. A few years back, I began knitting "Chemo Caps" and donating them to the Commonwealth Cares "Chemo Caps for Kids" initiative. One memorable year, we teamed up with Pioneer Yarn, our local yarn store, and knitted about 200 chemo caps together. They turned out incredibly cute and the process was loads of fun.

Find something that inspires you today and dedicate some time to developing your passion. It's a joyful and rewarding way to make a difference!

Overcoming Challenges

Embarking on new hobbies and interests can sometimes be a rocky journey. You might find that the guitar is tougher to master than you recall, or your initial forays into painting may not quite live up to your expectations (tip: check out free lessons on YouTube to get past these hurdles!). While these challenges can be daunting, it's vital to see them as part of the adventure rather than setbacks.

However, the real magic lies in starting these activities long before you retire. Most people approach retirement with apprehension, unsure of how they'll fill their days. By beginning to explore and enjoy these passions early, you not only enrich your present life but also pave the way for a retirement filled with activities you love. This proactive approach removes the fear of the unknown, replacing it with excitement for continued growth.

The beauty of retirement should not be the sudden abundance of time, but rather the continuation of a life already rich with purpose and joy. When you eventually retire, you won't be stepping into a void, but continuing a journey that's already well underway. This shift in perspective allows you to progress at your own pace, free from the pressure of deadlines or expectations, fully embracing the leisure and liberty that retirement offers.

Exploring New Avenues and Learning New Skills

Retirement is also the perfect stage to venture into entirely new territories. With time as your ally, you can afford to be a beginner again. You could learn new skills — be they gardening, pottery, or gourmet cooking. Enroll in courses, join local clubs, or find online communities that share your newfound interest. Each new skill learned, or hobby embraced, adds another vibrant strand to the riches of your retirement life.

Turning Passions into Business

As highlighted in Chapter 2, retirement can also be an opportune time to channel your passions into entrepreneurial endeavors. Many retirees find fulfillment in turning a hobby into a thriving business. Whether it's crafting, consulting based on your professional expertise, or even starting a small café, this can be an incredibly rewarding way to blend passion with purpose. It's not just about financial gain but about creating a legacy and a sense of accomplishment.

Treat this entrepreneurial spirit as part of your portfolio of activities. It's a chance to apply your lifetime of skills and experience in a new, fulfilling context, to meet new challenges, and to continue to grow and contribute in meaningful ways.

Wanderlust Unleashed: Travel as a Cornerstone of Retirement

In the context of a portfolio lifestyle, travel becomes much more than just a leisure activity—it becomes a pivotal aspect of a rich and varied life. Often, the desire to explore the world is put on hold due to the demands of career and family commitments. However, as you transition into this new phase, the call of wanderlust becomes louder, urging you to explore, immerse, and discover.

Traveling in this stage of life is about turning each trip into a chapter of learning and joy. It's a chance to engage deeply with different cultures, learn new languages, and experience the world through a more relaxed and insightful lens. By integrating travel into your life before you retire, you ensure that it becomes a seamless part of your journey, enriching your experiences both now and in the future.

Embracing the World as Your Classroom

Retirement affords a unique opportunity to travel in ways that were never possible during the working years. No longer confined by limited vacation days or the need to cater to everyone's preferences, you can now design travel experiences that resonate with your personal interests and pace. Whether it's a leisurely river cruise through Europe, a wildlife safari in Africa, or an immersive cultural experience in Asia, each trip adds to your personal growth and enrichment.

For many retirees, travel is about more than seeing new places; it's about engaging with the world in a deeper, more meaningful way. It's about learning from different cultures, understanding global perspectives, and connecting with people from walks of life vastly different from one's own. This kind of experiential learning enriches the soul and broadens the mind in profound ways.

The Joys of Slow Travel

One of the joys of retirement travel is the luxury of time. This opens the door to "slow travel" – a concept where you spend longer periods in one place, allowing for a deeper connection with the locale. Renting a villa in Tuscany for a month or wintering in a beach town in Mexico lets you live like a local, experiencing the rhythms of daily life that tourists rarely see. It's about savoring each moment, whether it's a leisurely meal with new friends or a quiet afternoon in a local café, watching the world go by. Getting there can also become more of a pleasure if you can use road, rail, or waterways instead of flying.

Planning Your Adventures

Effective planning is key to fulfilling travel in retirement.

This involves not just choosing destinations, but considering the best times to visit, understanding health and safety requirements, and budgeting for your adventures. Technology can be a great ally here, with travel apps and websites making it easier to research, plan, and even meet fellow travelers.

Consider also travel insurance, which becomes increasingly important as we age. It's not just about covering trip cancellations or lost luggage but ensuring access to quality healthcare should you need it abroad.

Guiding Tip: Consider Eco-Tourism

Consider embracing eco-tourism for your next adventure, a travel philosophy that not only offers unique and enriching experiences but also exemplifies sustainable tourism practices.

Eco-tourism focuses on minimizing environmental impacts while supporting conservation efforts and enhancing the well-being of local communities. This approach fits seamlessly into a portfolio lifestyle by promoting deep, meaningful interactions with nature and fostering respect for diverse cultures.

CONTINUED ON NEXT PAGE...

Guiding Tip: Consider Eco-Tourism

...CONTINUED FROM PREVIOUS PAGE

For example, imagine venturing into the lush rainforests of Costa Rica, where you can stay at eco-lodges that use renewable energy and local materials, reducing their carbon footprint. During your visit, you can participate in guided nature walks led by local experts who share insights into the region's biodiversity. These experiences not only enrich your understanding of the world but also contribute to the preservation of these precious ecosystems for future generations.

Orchestrating a Diverse Retirement Routine

In the harmonious joy of retirement, each day presents a new opportunity to compose a symphony of activities that resonate with your soul. The concept of a portfolio lifestyle extends beyond the mere accumulation of hobbies and interests; it's about orchestrating a daily routine that harmonizes the diverse elements of your life. This section is about finding that sweet spot where your activities blend seamlessly, creating a rhythm that is both energizing and fulfilling.

The Art of Balance

In creating your daily routine, balance is crucial. It's easy to overcommit or to lean too heavily into one type of activity. The goal is to weave a diverse yet coherent pattern that includes physical, mental, social, and relaxation components. Just as a symphony includes a variety of instruments and rhythms to create a beautiful piece, your retirement routine should include a variety of activities to create a fulfilling day.

Remember, rest and relaxation are as important as active pursuits. Ensure you allocate time for restful activities like reading, meditating, or simply sitting in your garden. This downtime is vital for rejuvenation and offers a moment to reflect and appreciate the richness of your retirement life.

Crafting Your Social Symphony

Just as no symphony can reach its full emotive power without the harmonious interplay of diverse instruments, a fulfilling retirement requires the vibrant melody of social connections. The beauty of incorporating varied social activities into your daily routine cannot be overstated. Engaging regularly with friends, family, and community groups not only enriches your life but is also essential for maintaining emotional well-being and health.

Consider the dynamic layers of a symphony—each instrument brings its unique sound, creating a richer, more compelling whole. Similarly, the different facets of your social life—from weekly lunches with lifelong friends to engaging discussions in a book club, or meaningful contributions through volunteering—each add significant depth and texture to your life's tapestry. These interactions are more than just pleasant diversions; they are crucial to a successful retirement, leading to enhanced health and greater overall happiness. By treating your social life like a well-conducted symphony, you ensure that your retirement is as enriching and fulfilling as a beautifully orchestrated piece of music.

The Agile Retiree: Mastering Flexibility and Adaptability

In a vibrant portfolio lifestyle, flexibility and adaptability are not just skills; they are art forms that the agile retiree masters. This mastery is crucial in a phase of life that's often wrongly stereotyped as rigid or set in its ways. Retirement, especially one that embraces a portfolio of diverse activities, requires an openness to change and a readiness to pivot when necessary. This section explores how retirees can cultivate and leverage these qualities to enhance their retirement experience.

Embracing Change as the New Constant

The first step to becoming an agile retiree is to embrace change as a natural and exciting part of life. Retirement is a significant transition, and it's normal for plans and interests to evolve over time. This might mean discovering new hobbies that replace old ones, finding unexpected opportunities for travel, or even relocating. The key is to view these changes not as disruptions but as opportunities for growth and enrichment.

Imagine a retiree who planned to spend their days golfing but discovered a passion for painting or a love for community theater. By embracing this change in interests, they open doors to new communities, learning experiences, and sources of joy.

Flexibility in Daily Life

Flexibility also applies to the structure of your daily life. While routines are beneficial, being too rigid can lead to missing out on spontaneous opportunities. It's about finding the right balance between a structured day and leaving room for impromptu experiences. This could look like having a few fixed activities each week, while keeping other days open for new adventures or simply following where the day takes you.

Adaptability is also about adjusting your expectations. Retirement might not look exactly as you envisioned, and that's okay. It's about making the most of the life you have, finding joy in the unexpected, and adapting your goals and activities to your current circumstances.

Guiding Tip: Your Greatest Asset

Adaptability is your greatest asset in retirement. Embrace change with a positive attitude and view unforeseen challenges as opportunities to learn and grow.

Staying Open to New Learning

Another aspect of agility in retirement is the willingness to learn and grow continuously. Embracing new technology can be particularly beneficial as we age, helping us stay connected with family and friends, and allowing us to pursue new interests. Learning new skills, taking up new sports, or adapting to new cultural environments, especially if you choose to travel or relocate, are all part of this journey.

The benefits of learning new technology are vast. It keeps our minds sharp, fosters independence, and helps us stay engaged with the world around us. Whether it's learning to use a smartphone, navigating social media, or mastering video calls, these skills can significantly enhance our quality of life. Technology also opens doors to a plethora of online courses and resources, enabling us to explore new hobbies and interests from the comfort of our homes.

My husband, Derek, still prefers to make a phone call and talk to someone rather than text or email. However, recently he's adopted a new approach by embracing these forms of communication as a new skill. Instead of feeling frustrated, he's proud of himself for learning to text or email. It's a mindset, really—being open to change and willing to embrace new ways of doing things. This adaptability not only keeps us mentally active but also boosts our confidence and sense of achievement.

Staying open to new learning means giving yourself the freedom to explore and the permission to be a beginner. There's joy in the process itself, in the gradual unfolding of your abilities and understanding. This mindset of continuous growth and adaptation can make retirement a vibrant, fulfilling chapter of life, rich with new experiences and connections. Embrace the journey of learning, and let it enhance your retirement in ways you might never have imagined.

Portraits of Diversity: Real-Life Embodiments of Portfolio Living

In the kaleidoscope of retirement, each person's story is a unique hue, contributing to the vivid panorama of portfolio living. This section paints portraits of individuals who have embraced this lifestyle, illustrating how diversifying activities in retirement can lead to fulfillment and joy. Their stories serve as inspirations, showcasing real-life embodiments of the principles we've explored.

Sally, the Renaissance Woman

Meet Sally, a retired engineer whose passion for learning didn't retire with her job. Post-retirement, she turned her attention to the arts, a field she had always admired but never explored. She started with painting classes, leading to a newfound love for art history. Now, she volunteers as a guide at a local art museum, sharing his enthusiasm and knowledge with visitors. Sally's days are a blend of creating art in her studio and immersing herself in the art community, a balance that keeps her mind active and her heart content.

The Community Connector: Emile's Encore Career

Emile's story is about turning professional expertise into community impact. After retiring from his role as a social worker, he now leads a community project that focuses on intergenerational learning. He coordinates programs where seniors teach skills like woodworking or knitting to younger generations. His retirement is driven by his passion for social work, continuing to contribute to his community in meaningful ways.

The Fitness Enthusiast Turned Coach: Ellen's Active Legacy

Fitness had always been a part of Ellen's life, but retirement gave her the opportunity to take this passion further. She became a certified yoga instructor, specializing in classes for seniors. Her classes are not just about fitness; they're a hub for socializing and building a community of health-conscious retirees. Ellen's retirement is an embodiment of her belief in active living, proving that age is no barrier to fitness and community building.

These portraits, each distinct and vibrant, reveal the limitless possibilities that a portfolio lifestyle offers. They are not just stories of individuals but are narratives of lives enriched by diverse pursuits. Sally, Emile, and Ellen exemplify how retirement can be a time of exploration, contribution, and growth.

Their experiences illuminate the path for those embarking

on their retirement journey, showing that this chapter of life can be as dynamic, colorful, and fulfilling as you choose to make it. In the portfolio of retirement, every activity, interest, and pursuit adds a unique dimension to your life, creating a retirement experience that is truly your own.

Economic Harmony: Financial Strategies for Sustaining Your Retirement Activities

Achieving economic harmony is crucial for sustaining the diverse range of activities that constitute a portfolio lifestyle. This section explores financial strategies to help ensure your retirement savings support both your basic needs and your passions. It's about balancing living your dreams and maintaining financial stability.

Budgeting for a Diverse Retirement

Start by outlining your regular expenses—housing, food, and healthcare. Allocate funds to your interests and hobbies, such as travel, classes, or starting a small business. Use budgeting tools or apps to track your spending, and review your budget regularly to stay on track. Flexibility is key; as your interests evolve, so might your spending patterns.

Creating Multiple Income Streams

In addition to pensions or savings, explore other income sources to enhance financial security and flexibility. Part-time work, consulting, or turning a hobby into a business can provide additional income and intellectual engagement. Rental income from property can also support your lifestyle and fund your interests. Diversifying income streams helps ensure financial stability and allows you to fully embrace a life of diverse experiences.

Planning for the Long Term

Consider the costs of healthcare, potential long-term care needs, and inflation. Planning for these eventualities will help ensure your finances remain robust throughout retirement. For a fuller discussion of these topics, refer to Chapter 8.

Living Within Your Means

Living within your means is vital to maintaining a vibrant and fulfilling portfolio lifestyle. Enjoy your hobbies and travel cost-effectively by traveling off-season or taking community classes. Sustainable financial decisions are crucial to avoid one of the biggest mistakes retirees make: spending more than their portfolio can support. By being mindful of your expenses and making smart financial choices, you can help ensure your retirement remains enjoyable and secure.

Have Fun

Start an 'adventure fund' specifically for your hobbies and passions. Regularly set aside a small amount to indulge in your interests without impacting your essential budget.

By managing your finances thoughtfully, you can ensure your retirement years are as fulfilling and vibrant as you envisioned, filled with the activities and pursuits that bring you joy and purpose. For more detailed financial strategies, see Chapter 8.

A Renaissance of Self: Continuous Growth and Learning in Later Life

Embracing a portfolio lifestyle in retirement is about more than filling time; it's about enriching the soul, expanding the mind, and continuously evolving. This section considers how retirees can foster this continuous growth, converting retirement into an era of personal renaissance.

Cultivating a Growth Mindset

The foundation of continuous growth in retirement is cultivating a growth mindset. This perspective views challenges as opportunities and failures as lessons. It's about looking at retirement not as a time to settle but as a time to explore, experiment, and expand. Whether it's learning a new language, picking up a new skill, or diving into an unfamiliar subject, the growth mindset propels you forward, turning each day into an adventure in learning.

Consider Helen, a retired teacher who turned her love for literature into leading book clubs at her local library. She not only shares her passion but also challenges herself by choosing diverse genres and themes, ensuring her learning never stagnates.

Maintaining Physical and Mental Fitness

Continuous growth also encompasses physical and mental fitness. Engaging in physical activities like yoga, hiking, or dance keeps the body active, while pursuits like puzzles, games, or writing keep the mind sharp. This holistic approach to health is essential for enjoying a fulfilling and active retirement.

A renaissance of self in retirement is about seeing this period as a time of flourishing and growth. It's about painting your retirement canvas with broad strokes of learning, experiences, and engagements. In doing so, you not only enrich your life but often those around you. Embrace this renaissance with curiosity, enthusiasm, and an open heart, and watch as your retirement morphs into an ongoing journey of discovery and personal evolution.

Composing Your Retirement Masterpiece

As we draw the curtain on this chapter about embracing a portfolio lifestyle in retirement, it's time to reflect on the beautiful and intricate masterpiece that you are composing with your life. This journey through diversifying activities in retirement is more than a guide; it's an inspiration to craft a retirement that is as unique and multifaceted as you are.

Guiding Tip: It's Personal

Remember, your retirement is a personal masterpiece that you're free to repaint and adjust as you go along. It's never too late to add new colors, themes, or directions to this work of art that is your life.

Embracing the Possibilities

Envisioning "The Early Start Retirement Plan" through a portfolio lifestyle allows you to see retirement not as a distant phase, but as a vibrant canvas being painted every day. Each new interest pursued, every travel adventure embarked upon, and each learning experience undertaken, paints a vibrant stroke on this canvas. Your retirement evolves into a dynamic and colorful masterpiece, a true expression of your deepest passions, curiosities, and aspirations.

The Harmony of Balance

As you weave various activities into your retirement, remember the importance of balance. Like a well-composed symphony, retirement should harmonize the tranquil with the active, the solitary with the social, the familiar with the novel. This balance ensures that each day is not just filled but is fulfilling, bringing satisfaction and joy in equal measure.

A Journey of Self-Discovery

Retirement is not just about rediscovering who you were before the demands of career and family took center stage; it's also about discovering who you can still become. This period is ripe for exploration – of new skills, new knowledge, and perhaps even new aspects of yourself. Let this time be a testament to your unending capacity for growth and development.

Your Masterpiece, Your Retirement

As you move forward in your retirement, armed with the insights and inspirations from this chapter, remember that your retirement is yours to design. It can be as vibrant, as serene, as adventurous, or as creative as you wish it to be. Each day offers a new opportunity to add to your masterpiece, to make your retirement not just a time of life but a work of art.

In composing your retirement masterpiece, embrace the portfolio lifestyle with all its diversity and richness. Let it be a reflection of all that you are and all that you wish to be. As I always say, "Retirement is not just a phase of life; it's a space for living life to its fullest." So, take the brush, the pen, the instrument of your choice, and create the retirement masterpiece that you've always dreamed about.

A Portfolio Lifestyle is about embracing the full spectrum of possibilities that retirement offers. It's about seeing this phase not as a winding down but as an opportunity to diversify and enrich one's life with a variety of activities – from leisure and travel to learning and volunteering, from creative pursuits to perhaps even a second career. Each of these elements contributes to a balanced and satisfying life, ensuring that retirement is a time of growth, joy, and fulfillment.

We've seen how integrating different interests and hobbies, and maintaining a blend of relaxation and engagement, can lead to a more contented and enriched life. This approach challenges the conventional view of retirement as a period of inactivity, urging us to see it as an opportunity for continued development, exploration, and contribution.

Consider how a Portfolio Lifestyle might resonate with your aspirations. Think about how you can blend various activities and interests to create a retirement that is not only meaningful and enjoyable but also reflective of who you are and what you love.

The Early Start Retirement Plan: Crafting a Portfolio of Passions

Retirement through a portfolio lifestyle is a journey marked not by a single path but by many—a journey as unique and individual as you are. It's an invitation to live your retirement years with richness and diversity, enriching your life and inspiring those around you. Embrace this journey with an open heart and an adventurous spirit, and let your retirement be a time of vibrant exploration and heartfelt enjoyment.

CHAPTER FIVE

Mini-Retirements: Taking Extended Breaks Along The Way

I magine a life where the path to retirement is enriched with intervals of exploration, relaxation, and personal growth. These aren't just brief vacations but substantial breaks—mini-retirements where you step away from daily routines to dive into new experiences or simply enjoy the pleasure of relaxation. This philosophy challenges the traditional norms, integrating periods of rest and adventure throughout your working life, encouraging you to recuperate, rejuvenate, recharge, and reevaluate at various stages, not just at the career's end.

The essence of mini-retirements is about pausing to reflect on your current life and future aspirations. These breaks allow you to explore, pursue hobbies, volunteer, learn new skills, or spend quality time with loved ones—activities often sidelined during the busy years of career and family building.

To make these mini-retirements a feasible part of your life, it requires thoughtful planning and funding. Balancing the freedom they offer with the responsibilities of career and financial stability needs a flexible mindset and creative planning.

By embracing mini-retirements, we challenge the conventional wait to enjoy life only at retirement and propose an alternative: a life where pleasures and discoveries are evenly distributed across our years, allowing us to live fully at every stage.

The Mini-Retirement Philosophy

At its core, the philosophy of mini-retirements is about flexibility and intentional living. It's a recognition that life's journey need not be a relentless march to a distant retirement goal but can include meaningful and enriching experiences along the way. These breaks offer opportunities to travel, pursue hobbies, volunteer, or simply take time to reflect and reset. They are a proactive approach to prevent burnout, maintain enthusiasm for work, and keep life fresh and fulfilling.

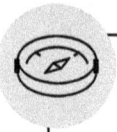

> **Guiding Tip:** *Early Start Retirement* as an Intermittent Lifelong Experience
>
> Mini-retirements challenge the conventional retirement model that suggests a linear path: work diligently for several decades and then step into a life of leisure around the age of 65.
>
> CONTINUED ON NEXT PAGE...

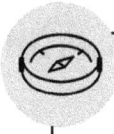

> **Guiding Tip:** *Early Start Retirement* as an Intermittent Lifelong Experience
> ...CONTINUED FROM PREVIOUS PAGE
>
> This newer approach intersperses working with chunks of time dedicated to rest, adventure, and self-discovery. It's a rhythm that recognizes the value of stepping back periodically to recharge and realign with your evolving passions and aspirations. Start retiring now! But plan first.

Contributing to Personal Growth and Well-Being

One of the most profound aspects of mini-retirements is their contribution to personal growth and well-being.

Imagine a corporate executive who takes a six-month break to volunteer in wildlife conservation, or a teacher who spends a year traveling the world. These experiences can really change their view of work and life, infusing them with renewed purpose and energy.

This flexible approach to retirement planning also acknowledges the changing nature of career and life expectations. People are living longer, healthier lives, and the desire to continue growing and learning doesn't wane with age. Mini-retirements offer a way to distribute the rest and rejuvenation typically reserved for traditional retirement throughout one's life, providing intervals to recharge and pivot as personal and professional needs evolve.

Planning and Funding Multiple Retirements

Embracing the concept of mini-retirements requires a strategic approach to planning and funding. Here, we consider the practical aspects of making these intermittent sabbaticals a reality.

The key to successfully implementing mini-retirements lies in thoughtful financial planning. This approach goes beyond saving for a singular retirement at the end of your career. Instead, it involves creating a financial roadmap that accommodates multiple breaks.

Consider establishing a dedicated savings plan for your mini-retirements, similar to setting aside funds for a major purchase or event. This could involve regular contributions to a separate savings account or investing in short-term, easily accessible assets that can fund your breaks.

Budgeting for a mini-retirement is an exercise in precision. It requires an accurate estimation of the costs involved, including living expenses, travel costs, health insurance, and any loss of income during the break. Crafting a detailed budget helps in understanding the financial implications of your time off and ensures that your mini-retirement is both enjoyable and financially sustainable.

One way to support your mini-retirements financially is to generate passive income. This could include rental income from property, dividends from investments, or earnings from business activities. Some individuals also opt for freelance or consulting work during their mini-retirements, blending leisure with productive work that generates income.

Guiding Tip: Become a Digital Nomad

Many countries offer digital nomad visas, which allow remote workers to live and work in the country for a temporary period; usually up to six-months or a year. At the time of writing there were about eight such destinations in each of Central-and-South America, the Caribbean, and Asia; and more than twenty in Europe.

If you are considering this, factors to check out include the cost of living, internet speed and reliability, climate, culture, and visa requirements.

This is a great way to immerse yourself in a different culture. It also creates an excellent opportunity to find out if the location might make a good retirement home (see Chapter 3).

Visit www.EarlyStartRetirement.com to learn more about becoming a Digital Nomad.

In today's evolving work landscape, many find opportunities for mini-retirements through flexible work arrangements. This could involve negotiating sabbaticals with your employer, transitioning to part-time work, or engaging in project-based work that allows for extended breaks. Understanding and negotiating these arrangements can be a key component of your mini-retirement planning.

Given the complexity of planning and funding multiple retirements, seeking advice from financial advisors can be immensely beneficial. A professional can help tailor a financial strategy to your specific needs, ensuring that your mini-retirements are feasible and align with your overall financial health. With careful planning, these mini-retirements can enrich your life, providing opportunities for growth and rejuvenation that enhance both your career and personal life.

The Art of Juggling Mini-Retirements and Work

The allure of mini-retirements lies in their rhythm, a dance between periods of work and rejuvenating breaks. This rhythm, however, brings with it the challenge of moving smoothly between the two contrasting phases. In this section, we'll explore how to gracefully move between the worlds of work and mini-retirements, ensuring each phase complements the other.

The key to a smooth transition lies in preparation. Before embarking on a mini-retirement, it's crucial to set the stage for your return to work. This might involve discussing your plans with employers or clients, delegating responsibilities, and setting clear expectations about your availability. It's also wise to consider how your time off might impact your career trajectory and prepare accordingly. For those self-employed or running their businesses, it's about ensuring operations can continue in your absence, perhaps by automating systems or hiring temporary help.

Reintegrating into the workforce after a mini-retirement also requires a strategic approach. Start by easing back into work mode a few weeks before your break ends. This could mean updating yourself on industry developments, reaching out to your network, or simply setting up your work schedule. For those employed, touching base with colleagues and supervisors ahead of your return can make the transition smoother.

It's also important to manage expectations—both your own and those of your colleagues or clients. Acknowledge that it might take a moment to regain your professional momentum and allow yourself the grace to ramp up gradually.

The period after a mini-retirement is ripe for reflection. It's a time to assess what you've learned during your break and how these insights can be applied to your work. Perhaps your travels have sparked new ideas, or your volunteer work has given you a fresh perspective. Integrating these experiences into your professional life can enrich your work and enhance your job satisfaction.

Maintaining Professional Relevance

One of the challenges of frequent transitions is maintaining professional relevance. This means staying updated with industry trends, upskilling, and nurturing your professional network even while on break. Consider dedicating some time during your mini-retirement for professional development— this could be through online courses, reading, or networking.

Be flexible. Your career path after a mini-retirement might look different—perhaps more aligned with your evolved interests and values. Be open to these changes, as they often lead to more fulfilling and engaging work experiences.

Guiding Tip: Everyone has Changed!

If your work environment and colleagues seem different when you return from a mini-retirement, stop and think. It is probably you that changed. You are likely to be a different person after an adventurous interlude, especially if you ventured into new cultures, embraced learning, or engaged in deep introspection. Remember also that some people might be jealous of your dazzling experience. You might need to lean heavily on your EQ and soft skills.

CONTINUED ON NEXT PAGE...

Guiding Tip: Everyone has Changed!

...CONTINUED FROM PREVIOUS PAGE

Obviously, mastering the transition between work and mini-retirements is a balancing act that requires planning, self-awareness, and adaptability. It's about ensuring that each phase – work and rest – enriches the other, contributing to a well-rounded, satisfying professional and personal life. By embracing this art of transitioning, you can make mini-retirements a harmonious and integral part of your life's journey.

Crafting Fulfilling Experiences During Mini-Retirements

The essence of mini-retirements lies not merely in taking a break from work but in how these intervals are spent. Each mini-retirement can offer experiences that are both fulfilling and enriching. There is an art in crafting these experiences to ensure that every mini-retirement becomes a memorable chapter in the story of your life.

The journey of a fulfilling mini-retirement begins with setting clear goals and intentions. Ask yourself what you hope to achieve during this time. Is it relaxation, exploration, learning new skills, or contributing to a cause? Defining your objectives provides direction and purpose to your break, turning aimless days into rewarding experiences.

Consider writing down your goals, no matter how big or small. Whether it's learning to cook Italian cuisine in Tuscany, writing the first chapter of your novel, or simply spending quality time with family, having a tangible list of objectives can serve as a guide and a motivator.

Once your goals are set, plan activities that align with these aspirations. This might involve research, such as finding courses, travel destinations, or volunteer opportunities that resonate with your interests. The beauty of mini-retirements is the freedom they offer to explore diverse activities—from adventurous travel and creative workshops to serene retreats and community projects.

Remember, flexibility is key. While it's important to have a plan, allow room for spontaneity and unexpected opportunities. Sometimes, the most memorable experiences are those that are unplanned. Think about what you are aiming for:

- **Recharging:** Mini-retirements create an environment for recharging both physically and mentally. Incorporate activities that promote relaxation and wellness. This could be practicing yoga, meditating, engaging in physical activities, or simply enjoying the tranquility of nature. The change of pace can rejuvenate your energy and provide a fresh perspective on life.
- **Pursuing Personal Passions:** Mini-retirements offer the perfect opportunity to jump into personal passions that you may not have time for during regular work periods.

This is the time to indulge in hobbies or interests that you are passionate about but have put on hold. Whether it's painting, birdwatching, or studying history, immersing yourself in these passions can be deeply fulfilling and a significant source of joy.

- **Learning and Personal Growth:** Embrace the occasion for learning and personal growth during your mini-retirements. This could mean enrolling in educational courses, learning a new language, or acquiring a new skill. Such pursuits not only keep the mind active but also contribute to a sense of achievement and self-improvement.

Crafting fulfilling experiences during mini-retirements is about more than filling time; it's about enriching your life. It's a chance to step out of the ordinary, to explore, learn, relax, and grow. Each mini-retirement is a unique opportunity to add depth, joy, and meaning to your life, ensuring that every break contributes to your personal narrative in a significant and memorable way.

Avoiding Common Pitfalls and Challenges

Embarking on a journey of mini-retirements is akin to charting unexplored territory—it's exciting, invigorating, but not without its challenges. While these extended breaks offer enriching experiences, they also come with potential pitfalls that need careful navigation. Let's look at some common challenges associated with mini-retirements and consider strategies to avoid or overcome them. I want to ensure that your journey is as smooth as it is fulfilling.

- **Maintaining Financial Security:** Balancing dreams with reality is crucial when planning mini-retirements. Ensure you have a robust financial plan in place. This includes meticulous budgeting, dedicated savings for travels, wise investments, and establishing passive income streams. These breaks should not jeopardize your long-term financial stability or retirement goals.

- **Reintegration into the Workforce:** Seamlessly re-entering the workforce after a break can be challenging. Maintain professional contacts and stay updated on industry trends. Consider freelance or part-time work during your mini-retirements to keep your skills sharp and resume current. Show potential employers or clients that you've used your time off productively.

- **Maintaining Relationships and Social Ties:** Extended breaks can strain personal relationships. Clear communication is vital. Share your goals and aspirations, and make an effort to maintain connections through regular updates, digital communication, or planning for loved ones to visit or join part of your journey.

- **Managing Health and Well-being:** The excitement of mini-retirements should not compromise your health. Plan for healthcare coverage, especially if traveling abroad. Keep up with regular health check-ups and maintain a healthy lifestyle, even when away from your normal routine.

- **Dealing with Uncertainty and Expectations:** Mini-retirements often involve stepping into the unknown. Embrace this uncertainty as part of the experience. Manage your expectations and be prepared for plans to change. Flexibility and adaptability are your greatest assets in navigating the unexpected.
- **Avoiding Over- or Under-Planning:** Striking a balance between planning and spontaneity is essential. Over-planning can lead to a rigid, less enjoyable experience, while under-planning may result in missed opportunities or unnecessary stress. Plan the essentials but leave room for unexpected adventures.

Avoiding the pitfalls of mini-retirements requires a blend of careful planning, open communication, and a flexible mindset. By being mindful of these challenges and preparing for them, you can ensure that each mini-retirement enriches your life with minimal stress. Embrace these breaks as opportunities for growth, learning, and rejuvenation, and they will become invaluable chapters in your life's story.

· · · · · · · · · · · · · · · · · · · ·▶

Case Study: The Andersons' Family Adventure

In "The Early Start Retirement Plan," we emphasize the importance of living fully in the present. This section is dedicated to a real-life story that inspires and demonstrates the transformative impact of mini-retirements.

Sailing Around the World: The Andersons' Story

Meet the Andersons—an upper-income family with two daughters. Believing that their daughters would learn more through real-world experiences than in a traditional classroom, the Andersons decided to take a year-long mini-retirement to sail around the world. They had a boat built specifically for their adventure and set off on a journey that would enrich their lives in unimaginable ways.

Before embarking on their voyage, the Andersons meticulously planned their trip, ensuring financial stability by setting aside a dedicated savings account and establishing passive income streams. They also researched educational resources to keep their daughters' studies on track, incorporating a blend of homeschooling and hands-on learning experiences.

As they sailed from port to port, the Andersons immersed themselves in diverse cultures, languages, and environments. Their daughters learned geography by navigating the seas, history by visiting ancient ruins, and biology by exploring marine life. The family bonded over shared challenges and triumphs, from navigating rough waters to discovering hidden coves.

Throughout their journey, the Andersons maintained connections with friends and family through regular updates and digital communication. They also made new friends in the various communities they visited, enriching their social ties and creating a global network of connections.

The experience was transformative. The daughters gained a

broader perspective on the world, enhanced problem-solving skills, and a deep appreciation for different cultures. The parents found joy in watching their children thrive in this unconventional learning environment and cherished the time spent together as a family.

Upon returning, the Andersons seamlessly reintegrated into their professional and academic lives. The journey left them with a treasure trove of memories, strengthened family bonds, and a renewed sense of adventure and curiosity. They often share their story to inspire others to consider how a well-planned mini-retirement can provide invaluable life experiences and deepen family connections.

This compelling story of the Andersons showcases how mini-retirements can be creatively and feasibly integrated into your life journey. With thoughtful planning and a spirit of adventure, you too can embark on enriching and transformative experiences that enhance the quality and richness of your life.

· ▶

Managing Relationships and Social Responsibilities

Maintaining strong relationships and fulfilling social responsibilities is also crucial. Communicate openly with loved ones about your plans and involve them in your journey where possible. If you have dependents, consider their needs and how your mini-retirements align with your responsibilities towards them.

Guiding Tip: It's An Art, Not a Science

Balancing the immediate desires of mini-retirements with long-term life goals is an art
form. It requires careful financial planning,
career strategizing, personal growth considerations, and maintaining strong relationships.
By finding this balance, you can ensure that
your mini-retirements are not just escapades
but meaningful interludes that contribute to
the grand narrative of your life.

Communicating the Mini-Retirement Approach to Others

When you embrace the concept of mini-retirements, a vital
aspect to consider is how you communicate this unconventional
approach to those around you. This may include family, friends,
colleagues, or even your broader social circle. Understanding
how to articulate your choices effectively can help in gaining
support and reducing misunderstandings. Let's explore the
nuances of conveying the essence of mini-retirements to others.

Initiating conversations about your mini-retirement plans
can be met with curiosity or concern. The key is to express
your vision clearly and confidently. Articulate why this path
is important to you, what you hope to achieve, and how it
aligns with your broader life goals. When others understand
that these are not merely extended vacations, but purposeful

intervals aimed at personal growth and exploration, they are more likely to be supportive.

Addressing Concerns and Misunderstandings

Be prepared to address concerns, especially from those closest to you. Family members may worry about financial stability or the impact on your career. Colleagues might question how your absence will affect workplace dynamics. Listen to their concerns empathetically and provide reassurance by explaining your plans, how you've prepared, and how you intend to manage the potential impacts.

Share the broader benefits of mini-retirements, not just for yourself but for your relationships and professional life. Explain how these breaks can lead to enhanced creativity, increased productivity, and a renewed perspective. For family and friends, emphasize how this approach can make you more present and engaged in your relationships, and for colleagues, highlight the fresh insights and skills you will bring back to the workplace.

Setting Expectations and Sharing

It's important to set realistic expectations about your availability and commitments during your mini-retirements. Make it clear if you plan to disconnect entirely or if you'll be available for occasional check-ins. Setting these boundaries early helps manage expectations and reduces the likelihood of misunderstandings or resentment.

Keep the lines of communication open, both before and during your mini-retirements. Regular updates can help maintain connections and reassure your loved ones. Sharing your experiences and learnings can also inspire others to consider how mini-retirements might fit into their own lives.

Effectively communicating the mini-retirement approach requires clarity, empathy, and openness. It's about sharing your vision and the thoughtful planning that goes into it, addressing concerns, and setting clear expectations. By doing so, you pave the way for understanding and support from those around you, enhancing your ability to fully embrace and enjoy your mini-retirements.

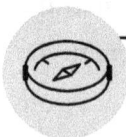

Guiding Tip: Use Stories & Examples

Sharing stories or examples of others who have successfully taken mini-retirements can be a powerful way to illustrate the concept. Whether it's a friend who returned from a mini-retirement with a new business idea or a public figure who speaks about the benefits of sabbaticals, these stories can serve as relatable and inspiring examples.

Reflection and Personal Growth Through Mini-Retirements

Time away from routine offers a fertile ground for self-discovery, personal development, and a deeper understanding of one's desires and aspirations. Use the following thoughts to help maximize the benefits you can reap.

Cultivating Self-Awareness

One of the greatest gifts of mini-retirements is the opportunity for introspection. Away from the daily grind, you can pause and ponder life's bigger questions: What brings me joy? What are my values? What legacy do I want to leave? This time for reflection can lead to significant insights about your life direction, helping you make more informed choices about your future, both personally and professionally.

Growth through New Experiences

Each mini-retirement is an opportunity to step out of your comfort zone. Whether it's learning a new language in a foreign country, volunteering in a different community, or simply dedicating time to a long-neglected hobby, these experiences broaden your horizons. They challenge you to grow in ways you may not have in your regular environment, fostering adaptability, resilience, and openness to new perspectives.

Documenting the Journey

Keeping a journal during your mini-retirements can enhance the reflective process. Writing about your experiences, feelings, and learnings helps solidify these insights, making them more tangible and actionable. It also serves as a wonderful memoir of your journey, a testament to your growth and adventures.

Realigning Life Goals

Mini-retirements can serve as checkpoints to reassess and realign your life goals. They provide the space to evaluate your current path and make adjustments if needed. Perhaps you discover a newfound passion that you want to integrate into your career, or you realize the importance of dedicating more time to family and relationships. These breaks can be pivotal in ensuring your life aligns with your evolving priorities.

Enhancing Well-Being

Beyond personal growth, mini-retirements can significantly enhance your overall well-being. They offer a respite for mental and physical rejuvenation, reducing stress and improving health. This revitalization can lead to a more fulfilling life, where you're not just surviving but thriving.

Sharing and Inspiring

Finally, your mini-retirement experiences can inspire and impact others. By sharing your stories, learnings, and other benefits, you can motivate those around you to consider their paths and possibilities. Your journey can be a catalyst for change, not just in your life but in the lives of others.

Guiding Tip: Beneficial for Everyone

In essence, mini-retirements are powerful tools for reflection and personal growth. They provide a unique opportunity to step back, reassess, learn, and grow.

Embracing these periods with intention and openness can lead to a richer, more fulfilling life, marked by continuous growth and deeper self-understanding. As you embark on these journeys, let each mini-retirement illuminate your path and guide you towards a life that resonates with your true self. It seems that mini-retirements could be beneficial for almost everyone. Be proud if you made even one happen.

Key Takeaways

As we reach the end of this exploration into the world of mini-retirements, it's clear that these extended breaks are more than just interludes in our career narratives; they are essential chapters in the story of our lives. Mini-retirements challenge the traditional script of working continuously until a conventional retirement age, offering instead a life where work and leisure dance in a more harmonious rhythm.

- o These periods of exploration, rest, and personal growth provide an opportunity to step back and view life from a different vantage point. They are a testament to the belief that our best years need not be deferred until the later stages of life but can be dispersed throughout our journey, enriching our experiences, and deepening our understanding of ourselves and the world around us.
- o As we have seen through the various sections of this chapter, "planning and executing" mini-retirements require thoughtful consideration – balancing financial needs, career trajectories, and personal aspirations. Yet, the rewards of such planning are immeasurable. They lie in the rejuvenation of our spirits, the broadening of our horizons, and the deepening of our relationships. They lie in the rediscovery of old passions and the exploration of new interests.

As you turn the page now, consider how the concept of mini-retirements might fit into your own life's story. Whether you're in the early stages of your career, in the midst of it, or contemplating the traditional retirement age, remember that life is not a race to the finish line. It's a journey to be savored, with moments of pause as essential as those of active pursuit.

Embrace these breaks as opportunities for growth, exploration, and rejuvenation, and watch as change your life into an enriching, multi-dimensional journey.

CHAPTER SIX

Sustainable Living: Off-the-Grid and Eco-Friendly Retirement

I n a world increasingly aware of environmental challenges, a growing number of retirees are turning towards lifestyles that embrace sustainability. Let's explore what it means to live sustainably in retirement, from integrating eco-friendly habits into everyday life, all the way through to embracing the communal spirit of off-the-grid living.

I will discuss the various facets of sustainable living in retirement, exploring the appeal of alternative living arrangements that offer harmony with nature and a fulfilling lifestyle. I will lead you through the practical aspects of creating and joining eco-friendly communities, understanding their environmental and personal benefits, and overcoming inherent challenges.

Through real-life stories and case studies, we will see how retirees are actively contributing to a greener planet while finding personal satisfaction. We also provide practical steps and strategies to help you embark on your sustainable living journey, ensuring your retirement benefits both you and the planet.

> **Guiding Tip: Retirement Reimagined in Harmony with Nature**
>
> Imagine a retirement that goes beyond leisure, one that embodies living responsibly, passionately, and sustainably. Let's reimagine retirement in harmony with nature.

Embracing Sustainable Practices

What does it mean to live sustainably, especially as a retiree? This concept extends beyond just recycling or using energy-efficient appliances; it's about a holistic approach to minimizing your environmental impact while maximizing life's quality. Sustainable living in retirement involves adopting practices that conserve resources, reduce carbon footprints, and minimize waste.

For many retirees, the decision to live sustainably often stems from a desire to leave a better world for future generations. It's an acknowledgment that our daily choices impact the planet. By adopting eco-friendly habits, retirees can play a crucial role in conserving natural resources and protecting the environment. In addition, it is very satisfying to trade the daily grind for the simplicity, tranquility, and beauty of nature.

The starting point is to integrate sustainable practices into your daily life in various ways. It can be as simple as reducing water usage, composting organic waste, or choosing renewable energy sources for their homes. Other practices include supporting local and sustainable agriculture, using public transportation, or driving electric vehicles. Each small step contributes to a larger impact on environmental conservation.

There's a profound joy and sense of fulfillment that comes from living sustainably. It's the pleasure of growing your own vegetables, the tranquility of living in an energy-efficient home, and the satisfaction of knowing each action contributes to a healthier planet. This lifestyle often leads to a deeper connection with nature and a more mindful way of living.

Guiding Tip: It's Not All or Nothing

I am not advocating leaving behind the luxuries of modern life. Luxury and off-grid are not mutually exclusive. Moreover, this is not an all or nothing choice. You can locate yourself anywhere along the spectrum from a simple change as mentioned in the text such as saving water, all the way through to full off grid living.

Tips for Getting Started

Here's an outline of ways to make your home eco-friendlier. If you have not done these things, doing it now can save you money too.

Conserving Water

- Fix leaky faucets and toilets: Even a small leak can waste a lot of water over time. Leaky faucets can waste up to 1 gallon of water per hour, and a leaky toilet can waste up to 200 gallons per day!
- Shorten showers: Aim for 5-minute showers instead of long ones.
- Install a low-flow showerhead: Low-flow showerheads can reduce water use by up to 50% without sacrificing water pressure.
- Turn off the faucet while brushing your teeth or shaving.
- Run full loads of laundry and dishes: This will help you use less water per wash cycle.
- Water your lawn and plants efficiently: Water early in the morning or evening to minimize evaporation. Use a watering can for targeted watering and avoid using sprinklers during windy days – see Garage Greening and Garden Glory on pages 150-151.

Conserving Energy

- Switch to LED light bulbs: LED bulbs use up to 90% less energy than traditional incandescent bulbs and last much longer.
- Turn off lights when you leave a room: This is a simple but effective way to save energy.
- Unplug electronics when not in use: Even electronics in standby mode can use energy. Use power strips and turn

them off completely when electronics are not in use.

- Adjust your thermostat: Lower the thermostat in the winter and raise it in the summer by a few degrees. You won't notice a big difference in comfort, but you can save a significant amount of energy.
- Air dry clothes whenever possible: Skip the dryer and hang your clothes to dry on a clothesline or drying rack. This is a free and eco-friendly way to dry your clothes.
- Use energy-efficient appliances: When replacing old appliances, look for models with the Energy Star label. These appliances are designed to use less energy.

Reduce Waste

- Recycle and compost: Recycling reduces the amount of waste that goes to landfills, and compost can be used to fertilize your plants.
- Buy products with minimal packaging: Avoid products with excessive packaging, which often ends up in landfills.
- Use reusable bags and containers: Avoid single-use plastic bags and containers by using reusable ones for shopping, groceries, and lunches.
- Buy in bulk: Buying in bulk can reduce packaging waste, but be sure you'll use everything before it expires.

Invest in Sustainable Features

- Install a programmable thermostat: This allows you to program your heating and cooling system to automatically adjust the temperature when you're away or asleep.

- Upgrade your windows and doors: Drafty windows and doors can let in a lot of heat or cool air, making your HVAC system work harder. Upgrading to energy-efficient windows and doors can help you save money on your energy bills.

- Install solar panels: Solar panels generate electricity from the sun, which can help you reduce your reliance on the grid and save money on your electricity bills.

- Battery backup system: A battery backup system can store solar energy so you can use it even when the sun isn't shining. This is a great option if you want to be more self-sufficient in terms of your energy needs.

- Graywater system: A graywater system collects wastewater from showers, sinks, and washing machines and reuses it for irrigation. This can help you conserve water and reduce your reliance on municipal water supplies.

Garage Greening

- Reduce, Reuse, Recycle: Declutter your garage and sort through items. Donate, sell, or recycle anything you no longer need. This not only frees up space but keeps items out of landfills.

- Green Cleaning: Use eco-friendly cleaning products that are non-toxic and biodegradable. These products are better for your health and the environment.

- Natural Light: If possible, add windows or skylights to

your garage to reduce reliance on artificial lighting during the day.

- Smart Storage: Utilize vertical storage solutions like shelves and hanging racks to maximize space and minimize clutter. This can also help prevent spills and leaks from reaching the floor.
- Rain Barrel Installation: Capture rainwater runoff from your roof in a rain barrel. This collected water can then be used for watering your plants, washing your car, or other non-potable purposes.
- Oil Recycling: Don't pour used motor oil down the drain! Find a local oil recycling center and dispose of it properly. Many auto parts stores accept used oil for recycling.

Garden Glory

- Embrace Native Plants: Choose plants that are native to your region. These plants are adapted to your local climate and require less water and maintenance.
- Attract Pollinators: Plant flowers that attract bees, butterflies, and other pollinators. These creatures are essential for a healthy ecosystem.
- Compost Magic: Create a compost pile or bin to turn your kitchen scraps and yard waste into nutrient-rich fertilizer for your garden.
- Mulch it Up: Apply a layer of mulch around your plants to retain moisture, suppress weeds, and regulate soil temperature.

- Water Wisely: Water your plants deeply and infrequently, rather than shallowly and frequently. This encourages deeper root growth and reduces water waste.
- Embrace Rainwater: Utilize a rain barrel system to collect rainwater for watering your garden.
- Natural Pest Control: Encourage natural predators like ladybugs and lacewings to help control garden pests. You can also use organic pest control methods like insecticidal soap or neem oil.
- Sustainable Lawns: Consider alternatives to traditional grass lawns. You could plant a native wildflower meadow, which requires less mowing and watering, or use drought-tolerant groundcovers.

By implementing some or all of these tips, you can make your home eco-friendlier and reduce your environmental impact. Remember, even small changes can make a big difference!

Exploring Off-the-Grid and Eco-Friendly Communities

As we dive into sustainable retirement living, let's explore off-the-grid and eco-friendly communities. These unique environments prioritize sustainability, self-sufficiency, and a deep respect for the environment.

Living off-the-grid means being disconnected from traditional public utilities, relying instead on renewable energy sources like solar or wind power, sustainable water sources, and organic waste management. This lifestyle fosters independence from mainstream energy grids and a closer connection to nature.

You can choose to live off-grid independently or join an eco-friendly community. These communities offer more than sustainable living practices; they provide a sense of belonging and shared purpose. Founded on principles of cooperative living, residents work together to maintain their environment and share resources, fostering a sense of connectedness with each other and the earth.

Intentional communities and co-housing represent eco-communities where residents actively choose to live according to specific sustainability values. These communities promote social interaction and shared responsibilities, from communal gardening to collective decision-making, shifting from individualism to a more collaborative way of life.

Building or joining an eco-friendly community can be an exciting prospect. These communities offer the opportunity to live in alignment with environmental values while enjoying camaraderie and shared purpose.

Building an eco-friendly community involves selecting a suitable location, planning sustainable infrastructure, and creating community guidelines reflecting shared sustainability goals. This process requires collaboration with architects, environmental experts, and future residents.

For those who prefer to join an existing community, research is key. Look for communities that align with your sustainability values and lifestyle preferences. Consider factors like location, community size, and governance model. Visiting these communities and interacting with current residents can provide valuable insights into life there.

One of the joys of eco-friendly communities is connecting with like-minded individuals who share a commitment to sustainability and a desire for a more connected way of living. Through community meetings, shared projects, or social events, these connections can be deeply enriching.

Guiding Tip: Embracing Sustainable Practices at Findhorn

The Findhorn eco-community, nestled in the north of Scotland, serves as a beacon for sustainable living and spiritual awakening. Originating in the 1960s, this vibrant community has flourished into a living model of harmony between humans and nature. My visit there was truly inspiring, especially seeing their commitment to practical sustainability measures like recycling envelopes to more communal efforts like cultivating extensive shared gardens. These gardens are not only spaces of natural beauty but also hubs of collective effort and ecological education. I am particularly excited about participating in their "Experience Week," which promises a deeper dive into sustainable living practices.

CONTINUED ON NEXT PAGE...

> ### Guiding Tip: Embracing Sustainable Practices at Findhorn
> ...CONTINUED FROM PREVIOUS PAGE
>
> This experience is designed to empower participants like myself with knowledge and practices that can be integrated into our daily lives, enhancing our connection to the environment and each other.

The Environmental and Personal Benefits of Sustainable Living

Sustainable living in retirement offers profound benefits, both for the environment and the individual. Embracing this lifestyle means playing an active role in conservation efforts, reducing environmental harm, and enjoying a healthier, more connected life.

Living sustainably has a direct, positive impact on the environment. It means reducing greenhouse gas emissions, conserving water, and minimizing waste. By choosing renewable energy sources and sustainable building materials, retirees can help preserve natural resources. Additionally, sustainable gardening practices contribute to biodiversity and the health of local ecosystems.

Beyond environmental contributions, sustainable living can significantly enhance personal well-being. It often leads to a healthier lifestyle, with increased physical activity and consumption of organic, locally-sourced food. Moreover, this lifestyle fosters a deep sense of purpose and fulfillment, knowing that one's daily choices are contributing to a greater good.

Challenges and Trade-offs

Adopting an eco-friendly/off-the-grid lifestyle is not without its challenges and trade-offs. If you are contemplating this shift, you must weigh the benefits against potential downsides and prepare for a different kind of living. Different, but not extreme. It all depends on where you locate yourself on the traditional to off-grid scale.

One of the main trade-offs in sustainable living might be adjusting to changes in comfort and convenience. Off-the-grid living might mean fewer modern amenities and a more hands-on approach to daily tasks. It's essential to assess how these changes align with your lifestyle preferences and adaptability.

Living in remote or eco-friendly communities can sometimes mean limited access to amenities like healthcare, shopping, or entertainment. Planning for these aspects is crucial, especially for healthcare needs in retirement.

The challenges of sustainable living can range from logistical or technical issues in setting up renewable energy systems to adapting to community living. Overcoming these obstacles often requires a combination of research, expert advice, and community support. It's also about embracing flexibility and a willingness to learn and adapt.

Case Studies and Real-Life Stories

In this section, we share inspiring stories of retirees who have embraced sustainable living practices, offering insights into the realities of this lifestyle choice.

John and Linda's Eco-Community Adventure

John and Linda retired in their early sixties and joined an eco-community focused on sustainable living and permaculture (permaculture is a system that mimics nature to create sustainable and productive human habitats). Their journey involved learning organic farming techniques and participating in community governance. Their story highlights the joys and challenges of adapting to a new way of living and the fulfillment of contributing to a sustainable future.

Emma's Off-the-Grid Transition

Emma chose to live off-the-grid in a solar-powered home in the mountains. Her story showcases the journey of setting up a self-sufficient home, the challenges she faced, and the peace she found in her closer connection to nature.

Emma's transition began with extensive research and planning. She selected a remote, picturesque location in the mountains, ideal for harnessing solar energy. The process of building her home was a learning curve, involving collaboration with architects and renewable energy experts to design a sustainable, energy-efficient structure.

Initially, Emma faced several challenges. Installing solar

panels and setting up a reliable water supply required significant investment and effort. She had to learn about maintaining these systems, from keeping the solar panels clean to ensuring her water filtration system was functioning correctly. Additionally, managing waste organically and adapting to a lifestyle without traditional utilities tested her resourcefulness and patience.

Despite the hurdles, Emma's determination paid off. Over time, she became adept at managing her self-sufficient home, finding joy in the simplicity and rhythm of off-the-grid living. Her daily routine involved tasks like gardening, tending to her home's systems, and enjoying the natural beauty surrounding her. The quiet, serene environment allowed her to reconnect with nature, providing a profound sense of peace and fulfillment.

Emma's story highlights the rewards of off-the-grid living. By embracing a sustainable lifestyle, she reduced her environmental footprint and discovered a deeper connection to the earth. Her journey serves as an inspiring example for those considering a similar path, demonstrating that with careful planning and perseverance, a self-sufficient, eco-friendly life is not only achievable but also incredibly rewarding.

Sustainable Living as a Long-Term Commitment

Committing to sustainable living in retirement is not just a one-time decision but a continuous journey. It involves staying informed, adapting to new technologies and practices, and finding ways to keep the commitment fresh and engaging.

Staying educated about environmental issues and sustainable technologies is key. This might involve attending workshops, joining environmental groups, or simply staying abreast of news and research in sustainability.

As technology and environmental strategies evolve, so too should your sustainable practices. This might mean upgrading to more efficient battery backup for solar panels, experimenting with new gardening techniques, or adjusting your lifestyle to reduce your environmental impact further.

Keeping the spirit of sustainable living alive requires ongoing motivation. Setting new goals, celebrating achievements, and connecting with like-minded individuals can help maintain your enthusiasm and commitment to this lifestyle.

Practical Steps Towards Eco-Friendly Retirement

Making the move to an eco-friendly retirement lifestyle can seem daunting, but with the right approach, it's entirely achievable. This section provides practical advice and steps to start implementing sustainable practices in your retirement (see also Tips for Getting Started on page 146).

- Start with manageable changes, such as reducing energy usage, recycling more, or choosing eco-friendly products. Small successes can build confidence and pave the way for more significant lifestyle changes.

- Focus on energy conservation in your home, such as by using LED lighting, energy-efficient appliances, and insulating your living space. Reducing waste by composting, recycling, and mindful consumption are also key steps.

- Adopt a mindset of mindful consumption. This means being more aware of the environmental impact of your purchases and opting for sustainable, local, and ethical products wherever possible.

- Utilize available resources and tools to assist in your transition. This might include online guides, community workshops, or consulting with sustainability experts.

Creating a Legacy of Environmental Stewardship

As we contemplate our impact and legacy, sustainable living offers a profound opportunity to leave a positive mark on the planet and future generations. Let's discuss how we can embrace environmental stewardship and create a "green legacy" that transcends our immediate circle.

We have a unique opportunity to influence younger generations by setting an example of sustainable living. By actively engaging in eco-friendly practices, we can inspire children, grandchildren, and our community to consider the environmental impact of their own choices. This ripple effect of influence is a powerful component of our green legacy.

Becoming involved in local environmental initiatives or advocacy groups can amplify our impact. Whether through volunteering for conservation projects, participating in community education programs, or advocating for environmental policies, these activities contribute to broader change and exemplify active, engaged citizenship in retirement.

We might possess a wealth of knowledge and experience that can be invaluable in environmental stewardship. Sharing this expertise through teaching, mentoring, or writing can help others follow the path to sustainability. Workshops on energy conservation, sustainable gardening, or eco-friendly home practices are just a few ways to impart our knowledge.

Living sustainably every day is perhaps the most direct way to build a green legacy. This involves adopting eco-friendly practices and making conscious choices that reflect environmental responsibility, such as supporting eco-friendly businesses, reducing waste, and conserving natural resources.

. . . . ▶

Key Takeaways

Embracing a sustainable retirement offers a pathway to a fulfilling, responsible, and impactful lifestyle. It's about aligning your retirement years with values of conservation, community, and stewardship.

Here are the key points:

○ **Align with Values:** Sustainable living reflects a commitment to conservation and stewardship, enhancing your quality of life while minimizing environmental impact.

○ **Maximize Quality of Life:** Sustainable practices lead to a healthier, more satisfying lifestyle and create a legacy that celebrates commitment to the planet and future generations.

○ **Assess and Adapt:** Evaluate your current lifestyle and identify areas for improvement. Small changes like reducing energy usage or major renovations for energy efficiency can make a significant difference.

○ **Stay Informed and Flexible:** Keep up with new sustainable technologies and practices. Be open to change as the world of sustainability evolves.

○ **Build Community:** Join groups of like-minded individuals to share advice, support, and encouragement on your journey toward sustainable living.

○ **Share Your Journey:** Inspire others by sharing your experiences. Your story can encourage a broader cultural shift towards sustainability.

○ **Leave a Legacy:** Create a legacy of care and respect for the planet, setting an example for future generations.

Initiating Sustainable Practices: Today's Steps Toward a Greener Retirement

Start integrating sustainable practices into your retirement plans today:

• Reflect on how your choices impact the planet and consider the legacy you aim to leave.

- Understand that every step towards sustainability, no matter how small, contributes to a healthier planet and a richer retirement.
- Join the community of retirees reshaping sustainable living by adopting eco-friendly practices and supporting local efforts.

Not for You? You Can Still Participate

Even if an off-grid or fully eco-friendly retirement isn't right for you, you can still help the planet and benefit yourself by adopting sustainable practices from the tips provided.

For more up-to-date information on eco-living and sustainable practices, visit our resource page at www.EarlyStartRetirement.com. Start your journey towards a sustainable retirement today—small, mindful actions can spark significant changes and leave a lasting legacy of stewardship and compassion.

CHAPTER SEVEN

Cultural Immersion: Engaging With the World

Retirement presents a unique opportunity to delve deeply into cultural immersion, a concept that goes beyond merely living abroad. While Chapter 2 explored the logistics and lifestyle of relocating to a new country, this chapter focuses on the profound personal growth and enrichment that comes from actively engaging with different cultures, whether at home or while traveling.

Cultural immersion is about integrating oneself into the fabric of another culture, understanding its nuances, and fostering genuine connections. This approach enriches life in ways that mere residency cannot, offering deeper insights and a more meaningful engagement with the world.

Incorporating cultural immersion into retirement can yield numerous benefits. It stimulates mental and emotional well-being by keeping the mind active and fostering a sense of curiosity and adventure. Engaging with new languages, traditions, and customs can significantly enhance cognitive function and provide a sense of accomplishment.

Cultural immersion promotes empathy and global awareness, helping retirees appreciate diverse perspectives and build a more inclusive worldview. These experiences can also lead to new social connections, reducing feelings of isolation and fostering a sense of community.

Immersion in Other Cultures

Cultural immersion can start now and right at home. Learning a new language, exploring cultural traditions through books and media, and attending local cultural festivals are great starting points. These activities allow us to dip our toes into different cultures without leaving our communities, fostering a sense of curiosity and respect for the diversity around us.

Learning a New Language: Language is a gateway to understanding culture. Enroll in a language course at a local community center or use online platforms like Duolingo, Rosetta Stone, or Babbel. Practicing a new language sharpens cognitive skills and enhances your ability to connect with native speakers on a deeper level during future travels. Engaging in language exchange programs can also provide a practical and enjoyable way to improve your skills while making new friends from different cultural backgrounds.

Exploring Cultural Traditions through Books and Media: Books, movies, and documentaries offer rich insights into the traditions, history, and daily life of other cultures. Reading novels by international authors, watching foreign films, or exploring documentaries about different countries can deepen your understanding and appreciation of the world's cultural diversity. These media allow you to experience the world from different perspectives, broadening your horizons and fostering empathy.

Attending Local Cultural Festivals: Many communities host cultural festivals that celebrate the traditions and heritage of various ethnic groups. These events are wonderful opportunities to experience new cuisines, music, dance, and crafts. Participate actively by engaging in conversations, asking questions, and trying out activities. These festivals are not just entertaining but also educational, providing firsthand exposure to the rich tapestry of global cultures.

Transformative Travel Experiences: While local activities offer valuable cultural insights, traveling to the country of interest can be truly transformative. Immersing yourself in a new environment allows for deeper engagement with the culture. Imagine savoring a freshly baked croissant at a quaint French patisserie, experiencing the serene beauty of a Buddhist temple in Thailand, or navigating the bustling streets of a Moroccan market. Each of these experiences enriches your understanding and appreciation of the world's diverse cultural landscapes.

Engaging with Locals: One of the most rewarding aspects of cultural immersion is connecting with local people. Whether through organized homestays, volunteer programs, or simply striking up conversations in a café, these interactions provide authentic insights into daily life, customs, and values. Building relationships with locals can lead to unforgettable experiences and lasting friendships, making your immersion journey deeply personal and enriching.

Volunteering Abroad: Volunteering in another country is a powerful way to immerse yourself in a new culture while making a positive impact. Whether teaching English, participating in conservation projects, or assisting in community development, these experiences offer a profound understanding of the local culture and challenges. Volunteering fosters a sense of purpose and connection, allowing you to contribute meaningfully to the communities you visit.

Joining Cultural Exchange Programs: Cultural exchange programs offer structured opportunities to live and work in a different country for an extended period. These programs are designed to facilitate deep cultural immersion, providing support and resources to help you integrate into the local community. Participating in a cultural exchange program can be a transformative experience, offering a blend of learning, adventure, and personal growth.

Personal Stories and Reflections: Reflecting on your experiences and sharing your journey with others can deeply enrich your cultural immersion. Consider keeping a journal, writing a blog, or creating photo albums to document your travels and insights. These records not only preserve your memories but also offer a creative outlet to process and celebrate your adventures. Sharing your stories with friends and family can inspire them to embark on their own cultural explorations, creating a ripple effect of curiosity and engagement.

My late cousin, Danny, was a master of this art. He traveled the world, immersing himself in unique and fascinating cultures. His regular posts on social media allowed us to share in his travels, offering glimpses into vibrant festivals, serene landscapes, and heartfelt encounters with locals. Through his photos and stories, Danny not only preserved his experiences but also sparked a sense of wonder and wanderlust in all of us.

By documenting and sharing your own cultural journeys, you too can create a lasting impact. Whether it's a blog that details your culinary adventures in Thailand or a photo album capturing the colorful markets of Morocco, these reflections can inspire and connect, turning your personal experiences into a shared celebration of the world's diverse cultures.

Engaging with Local Communities

Active participation in local community life greatly enhances the retirement experience, offering a sense of purpose and connection. Attending cultural festivals allows retirees to immerse themselves in local traditions, fostering a deeper understanding of the community's heritage and diversity. Joining community boards or neighborhood associations enables retirees to contribute their skills to local decision-making, providing a sense of accomplishment and belonging.

Volunteering, whether mentoring young people, participating in conservation projects, or helping at food banks, helps retirees stay active and engaged. These activities broaden social networks, enhance understanding of different perspectives, and promote physical and mental well-being. Retirement is not just a time for relaxation but an opportunity to enrich both personal lives and the lives of others.

Exploring the World

Cultural immersion in retirement can be profoundly enriched through homestays, where retirees live with local families and experience daily life firsthand. This immersive approach provides unique insights into the culture, traditions, and customs of the host country, far beyond what typical tourist experiences can offer. Homestays foster genuine connections, allowing retirees to form lasting friendships and gain a deeper understanding of the community.

While homestays are a highlight, other ways to engage with global cultures include attending cooking classes, participating in local festivals, and volunteering abroad. These activities enhance the travel experience by offering hands-on learning and personal interaction with locals.

Embracing slow travel, which involves longer stays in fewer locations, enhances the travel experience by fostering deeper connections with each destination and uncovering hidden gems. Aligning travel plans with personal interests and passions allows retirees to create fulfilling and memorable adventures. Integrating these immersive experiences into retirement leads to a richer and more meaningful connection with the world.

Creative Pursuits and Artistic Expression

Retirement is a time to explore creative endeavors that resonate with one's experiences and aspirations. Art transcends language and cultural barriers, connecting us on a fundamental level. Writing, painting, music, and dance are powerful outlets for cultural exploration. Joining multicultural art classes or workshops can provide new artistic techniques while experiencing diverse cultural perspectives.

Julia's Artistic Journey: After retiring from a fulfilling career in education, Julia decided to pursue her long-held passion for painting. She had always dreamed of immersing herself in the rich artistic heritage of Italy, so she embarked on a journey to the picturesque region of Tuscany. This decision marked the beginning of an extraordinary chapter in her life, filled with creativity, learning, and personal growth.

In Tuscany, Julia enrolled in a series of painting workshops led by renowned local artists. These workshops not only honed her technical skills but also exposed her to the unique styles and techniques of Italian art. Under the guidance of her mentors, Julia explored various mediums, from watercolor to oil painting, and experimented with different approaches to capturing the stunning landscapes and historic architecture that surrounded her. Each day brought new challenges and inspirations, deepening her appreciation for the artistic process.

Julia's journey extended beyond the canvas. She formed meaningful friendships with fellow artists from around the world who had also come to Italy to nurture their creative spirits. Together, they visited art museums, attended local cultural festivals, and shared countless meals, exchanging stories and ideas. These connections enriched her experience, providing a sense of community and shared purpose.

One of the highlights of Julia's time in Italy was the opportunity to showcase her work in a local gallery. Her paintings, inspired by the vibrant colors and serene beauty of the Tuscan countryside, received praise from both locals and tourists. This public recognition boosted her confidence and validated her decision to embrace her passion fully in retirement.

Julia's artistic journey in Italy exemplifies how retirement can be a time of rediscovery and personal fulfillment. By immersing herself in a new culture and dedicating herself to her art, she not only achieved personal growth but also contributed to the cultural exchange in her community.

Her story demonstrates that retirement is not an end, but a new beginning—a time to pursue dreams, explore new interests, and connect with others on a deeper level. Through her artistic endeavors, Julia found a renewed sense of purpose and joy, proving that retirement can be one of the most enriching and rewarding phases of our lives.

Embracing the Digital Revolution

Technology has revolutionized how we connect, learn, and engage with global cultures. Virtual museum tours allow us to visit renowned institutions from the comfort of our homes, offering immersive experiences that bring art and history to life. Online forums and social media platforms facilitate connections with people worldwide, fostering cultural exchange and understanding.

Learning new languages has never been easier with the plethora of online resources available. Apps and websites offer interactive lessons, helping users develop language skills at their own pace.

Exploring world religions or taking courses on international cuisine are also accessible through online platforms. These courses provide valuable insights into different cultural practices and traditions. By embracing these digital tools, we can broaden our horizons and enrich our understanding of the world.

Combining Cultural Immersion with Other Retirement Goals

Integrating cultural immersion into broader retirement plans can significantly enhance the overall experience. Starting the day with a language learning app can be a simple yet effective way to immerse yourself in a new culture. These daily practices not only improve language skills but also keep the mind sharp and engaged.

Attending a weekly cultural cooking class is another enjoyable way to blend cultural immersion with personal growth. Learning to prepare traditional dishes from different countries provides a hands-on approach to understanding diverse cultures. It also adds a social component, allowing you to meet new people with similar interests.

Volunteering for cultural exchange organizations offers an impactful way to give back while deepening your cultural understanding. These organizations often provide opportunities to mentor international students, assist in cultural festivals, or participate in community education programs. Such activities foster a sense of purpose and connection, making retirement a time of continuous growth and meaningful engagement.

Nurturing Personal Development Through Cultural Experiences

Cultural experiences in retirement foster reflection, adaptability, and empathy. Encountering different ways of life challenges preconceptions and inspires a deeper understanding of the world. Keeping a journal of cultural experiences and reflections can help process what you've learned and how it affects your view of the world and yourself.

• •▶

Key Takeaways

Embrace Cultural Immersion at Home: Start your journey

by learning a new language, exploring cultural traditions through books and media, and attending local cultural festivals. These activities can foster a sense of curiosity and respect for global diversity without leaving your community.

- **Engage Deeply with Different Cultures:** When traveling, opt for home stays, cooking classes, or local volunteer opportunities to gain genuine cultural insights. Slow travel encourages longer stays in fewer locations, allowing for deeper connections with each destination.

- **Pursue Lifelong Learning:** Retirement is an ideal time for intellectual enrichment. Utilize online courses, MOOCs, MasterClass, and TED Talks to explore new subjects and set personal learning goals. Community colleges and universities also offer special programs for retirees.

- **Participate in Local Communities:** Enhance your retirement experience by actively engaging with your local community. Attend cultural festivals, join community boards, and volunteer to foster a sense of belonging and purpose.

- **Leverage Technology:** Use digital platforms to connect, learn, and engage with global cultures. Virtual museum tours, online forums, social media, and language learning apps provide accessible ways to explore the world from home.

- **Plan Meaningful Adventures**: Align your travel plans

with personal interests to ensure fulfilling experiences. Whether it's exploring historical sites, hiking scenic trails, or attending local festivals, intentional travel enriches your retirement journey.

- ○ **Share Your Journey:** Document your cultural experiences through journals, blogs, or social media. Sharing your stories not only preserves your memories but also inspires others to embark on their own cultural explorations.

By embracing these key takeaways, you can make your retirement a time of rich cultural immersion and personal growth. Whether at home or abroad, the opportunities to learn, connect, and explore are endless, making this chapter of life truly fulfilling and rewarding.

CHAPTER EIGHT

Financial Strategies for Early Start Retirement Plans

Retirement paths are as diverse as the individuals embarking on them. Clearly, there can't be a one-size-fits-all approach to retirement financial planning. As we explore the various avenues that modern retirees are taking—from launching new ventures to living across continents—it becomes clear that financial strategies must be as unique as the dreams they support. I'll guide you through tailoring your financial planning to match your distinctive retirement goals, drawing on the wisdom of those who traced these paths before us.

Tailoring Financial Planning to Your Unique Goals

It's important to recognize that your financial strategy should mirror your personal aspirations and lifestyle choices. Whether your retirement vision includes volunteering in remote parts of the world, starting a foundation, or living a nomadic life abroad, each path requires a financial plan as unique as your individual journey.

> ### Guiding Tip: Early Start Planning for Today and Tomorrow
>
> The cornerstone of any successful retirement plan is starting early. Beginning your financial preparations ahead of time allows for a wider range of investment opportunities and more substantial growth potential. This proactive approach seeks not only to benefit your financial future but also afford you the flexibility to adapt as your retirement vision evolves, empowering you to live purposefully today and tomorrow.

I recommend starting by brainstorming all possible retirement goals. Dream big and be aspirational, what are all the possible ideas you have for ways to spend your time in retirement? Do you envision yourself starting a nonprofit? Perhaps spending half the year in another country? Seeing a baseball game at every stadium in the country?

Whatever your goals, being able to articulate the things you want to do will go a long way towards turning them into reality. As Dr. Joe Dispenza says, "Where our attention goes, grows." Clearly defining your retirement aspirations will help you map out a financial plan tailored to achieving them. This focused approach ensures that your resources are allocated effectively, making your dreams more attainable and your retirement more fulfilling.

Expanding Financial Strategies for a Fulfilling Retirement

The financial strategies for a fulfilling and adventurous retirement align with traditional planning, but they also go beyond merely covering basic living expenses. While it's essential to ensure stability and preserve capital for necessities like housing and groceries, it's equally important to plan for the experiences that make life exciting and meaningful. This chapter will explore how to integrate financial strategies that support not only your basic needs but also your aspirations for travel, starting a business, or engaging in philanthropic endeavors. By incorporating these elements into your financial plan, you can create a retirement that is set up to be both secure and enriching.

Consider the story of Alex and Jamie, who retired early to start a mobile veterinary service in underserved communities. Their financial plan included a detailed budget for startup costs, ongoing operational expenses, and a strategy for generating income through their services. They also built a safety net into their plan to cover unexpected expenses, ensuring their venture's sustainability.

Aligning your financial strategy with your retirement goals

involves a careful evaluation of your assets, income sources, and potential expenses. It also means being adaptable, recognizing that your goals may evolve over time.

Income Diversification

Diversifying your income sources during retirement is crucial for financial stability and peace of mind. Relying solely on a single source of income, such as Social Security or a pension, can leave you vulnerable to unexpected changes in your financial situation. By incorporating multiple income streams, such as part-time work, investments, rental properties, or side businesses, you create a safety net that can help you weather economic fluctuations and unexpected expenses. This diversified approach not only positions you for a potentially more secure financial future but also provides the flexibility to pursue your passions and enjoy a fulfilling retirement.

Budgeting for Your Dreams

Crafting a budget that reflects your individual and unique retirement aspirations is essential, whether that involves allocating funds for travel, charitable giving, or entrepreneurial ventures. To help you effectively manage and track your spending across various categories, I recommend using our free basic financial planning software. It's designed for flexibility and ease of use. Sign up today to start shaping a budget that turns your retirement dreams into reality!

Learn more at our resource center:
www.EarlyStartRetirement.com

Adapting to Change

A flexible mindset is your greatest asset in retirement planning. Regularly review and adjust your financial plan to ensure it continues to align with your goals, lifestyle changes, or shifts in the economic landscape.

In this initial exploration I've begun to unravel the complexity and excitement of planning for varying retirement paths. By aligning your financial strategies with your unique goals and staying adaptable to life's inevitable changes, you set the stage for a retirement filled with purpose, passion, and personal fulfillment. As we move forward, we'll dive deeper into generating and managing income, balancing sustainability with lifestyle choices, and much more, always with the aim of supporting your one-of-a-kind retirement journey.

Managing Income Streams and Expenses

For many entering their retirement today, the traditional pension or social security check may not fully cover the unique ambitions we set for our early start retirement. As such, creating diversified income streams becomes essential, especially for those interested in pursuing hobbies that turn into second careers, extensive travel, or philanthropy.

Diversification is your financial backbone. Embracing various income sources can provide the financial stability you need to pursue your dreams without worry. This could include part-time consulting within your professional expertise, investing in rental properties for passive income, or even developing online courses based on your skills and experiences.

One retiree, Elena, found success and fulfillment by turning her lifelong passion for photography into a source of income. By selling her photos online and teaching photography workshops, she not only supplemented her retirement savings but also engaged in work that she loves, proving that income in retirement can be both financially and personally rewarding.

Prioritize and plan. Start by distinguishing between your needs and wants. Priorities might include healthcare, housing, and essential living costs, while wants could encompass travel, hobbies, and luxury items. By understanding your priorities, you can better navigate financial decisions, ensuring you have the means to enjoy your pursuits without compromising your financial health.

> ### Guiding Tip: Your Interests Might Be the Key to Financial Independence
> Assess your hobbies and pastimes through a financial lens—could one of these passions offer a pathway to income generation in retirement?

Case Study: The Martins' Fulfilling Retirement

John and Sarah Martin started planning for their retirement early, understanding the importance of diversified income sources. After working for a publicly traded company for many years, they transitioned into consulting roles with their former employer. This consulting income, along with investment income and Social Security benefits, provided a steady financial base, allowing them to explore their passions with less financial stress.

With their financial foundation secure, the Martins embraced a lifestyle filled with extensive travel, both domestically and abroad. Their adventures not only enriched their lives but also served as inspiration for a series of novels that Sarah began writing. They combined their travels with family time, creating cherished memories with their children and grandchildren during vacations. By planning ahead and diversifying their income, including investments and Social Security, John and Sarah crafted a retirement designed to be both financially stable and deeply fulfilling.

· ▶

Embracing Tools and Resources

Fortunately, retirees today have access to a myriad of tools and resources to aid in financial planning. From budgeting apps that track spending in real time to financial advisory services that offer personalized advice, these tools can simplify the management of income and expenses, allowing you to focus more on enjoying retirement and less on financial logistics.

Stay Informed and Engaged. Review your financial situation regularly. Take notice of economic trends that could impact your income streams and investments. This proactive approach ensures you can adjust your plans as needed, maintaining financial stability while pursuing your non-traditional retirement path.

Guiding Tip: Tune Into the 'Ready to Retire!' Podcast

Enhance your retirement planning with insights from my podcast, 'Ready to Retire!'. With over 20 years of professional financial planning experience distilled into concise 15-20 minute episodes, you'll gain valuable knowledge on a wide array of topics tailored to make complex financial concepts accessible and actionable. Whether you're just starting to plan or refining your strategies, each episode is designed to guide you toward a more secure and fulfilling retirement. Start listening today to transform your financial future!

Links to the podcast are available at: www.EarlyStartRetirement.com or search "Ready to Retire" on your favorite Podcast App.

Balancing Financial Sustainability with Your Portfolio of Passions

The allure of a fulfilling retirement filled with passions— whether it's extending a lifelong hobby into a new career, dedicating oneself to philanthropy, or embarking on continuous global exploration—brings unique financial considerations. These aspirations, while immensely rewarding, require a nuanced approach to financial planning to ensure they are sustainable over the long term.

Embrace a holistic view of your finances. The first step is to adopt a comprehensive perspective on your financial health. This involves more than just assessing your savings; it's about understanding how each aspect of your financial life—expenses, income sources, investments, insurance, and estate planning—interacts to support your chosen lifestyle. A detailed financial plan that incorporates all these elements will provide a clear roadmap for maintaining financial stability while pursuing your passions.

For example, consider the long-term impact of your spending choices on your financial stability. Pursuing extensive travel or launching a new venture may have significant upfront costs. Planning for these expenses, while also considering their long-term implications, is crucial. Allocate funds in a way that allows for flexibility, enabling you to adjust your financial strategies as needed. This ensures that your retirement journey remains balanced and fulfilling, even as your interests and circumstances evolve.

Remember, flexibility in your financial plan allows you to adapt to both the expected and unexpected turns your retirement journey might take. This adaptability is key to enjoying a retirement that is both financially secure and deeply satisfying.

Challenges and Strategies

One of the major challenges in funding a diverse and fulfilling retirement is ensuring that your financial resources last as long as you need them. This concern is particularly pronounced for retirees who choose to retire early or invest heavily in passion projects.

Mitigate risks through planning. To safeguard against potential financial strain, establish a clear distinction between the funds allocated for essential living expenses and those earmarked for lifestyle aspirations. Consider creating a separate "lifestyle fund" that can be replenished over time through passive income streams or part-time work, reducing the risk of depleting your primary savings. This approach allows you to pursue your passions without jeopardizing your financial stability.

Managing debt wisely and maintaining a lean budget for day-to-day expenses can free up more resources for your lifestyle pursuits. Leveraging assets, such as downsizing your home or renting out property, can also provide additional funding without compromising your financial security.

Innovative financial planning—like setting up an "adventure fund"—can be the key to enjoying your unique retirement dreams with greater financial confidence. By implementing these strategies, you can navigate the challenges of a fulfilling retirement without jeopardizing long-term financial sustainability.

The Importance of Professional Guidance

Navigating the financial intricacies of an Early Start Retirement Plan often benefits from professional insight. A financial advisor who understands your lifestyle goals and has experience with long term retirement plans can offer invaluable guidance. They can help you craft a financial strategy that not only supports your lifestyle choices but also promotes your financial well-being over the long term.

Seek Advisors aligned with your vision. It's important to partner with professionals who respect your ideas and aspirations and are committed to helping you achieve them. Whether it's structuring investments for income generation, planning for tax efficiency, or managing healthcare costs, the right advisor can provide valuable guidance to help you work towards your retirement vision.

Achieving a fulfilling and financially sound retirement, especially when following a path less traveled, requires careful planning, a willingness to adapt, and sometimes, a bit of creativity in how we manage our resources. As we continue to explore the financial strategies that underpin alternative retirement paths, remember that the goal is not just to secure your finances but to empower your retirement dreams, making them both achievable and sustainable.

Exploring Investment and Savings Strategies

As you transition into retirement, your investment strategy should reflect your current risk tolerance and the need for income generation, balanced against the potential for growth. I recommend a diversified portfolio that includes a mix of asset classes. Fixed-income investments can provide regular income, while equities can offer growth potential to help combat inflation over time.

Innovative investment options such as socially responsible investments (now referred to as ESG investing) can align your portfolio with your personal values, adding a dimension of fulfillment that can transcend potential financial gain. These choices may not only support your financial goals but also contribute positively to the causes and ideals you care about.

Savings play a pivotal role in retirement, serving as both a safety net and a reserve for funding dreams and goals. Effective savings strategies in retirement should focus on liquidity and accessibility, ensuring that you have funds available for both expected expenses and unforeseen opportunities or challenges.

High-yield savings accounts, money market funds, and short-term bonds can provide relatively lower risk options for keeping your savings both accessible and productive. For those planning significant expenditures, such as starting a business or a major travel adventure, segmenting your savings into dedicated accounts can help track progress toward your goals while ensuring that you're not overextending your financial resources.

> ### Guiding Tip: Make Savings Happen
>
> Automating transfers to your savings accounts can help steadily build reserves for your retirement adventures, making it easier to manage finances and stay on track with your goals.

Risk Tolerance and Asset Allocation

Understanding and regularly reassessing your risk tolerance is crucial, especially if you plan on pursuing multiple passion projects during retirement. Your asset allocation—the mix of investments you hold—should reflect your risk tolerance, investment timeframe, and the financial demands of your chosen lifestyle.

As you progress through retirement, your financial situation, goals, and risk tolerance may evolve. Regular reviews of your investment portfolio and savings strategies are essential to ensure they remain aligned with your current needs and future aspirations. Adjustments may be necessary to respond to market changes, economic conditions, or shifts in your personal life and retirement goals.

Guiding Tip: Get a Checkup

Regular financial check-ups are as important as health check-ups in retirement. They help ensure your financial health remains robust and responsive to your life's changes and challenges.

As we navigate the intricacies of managing investments and savings for a retirement that breaks the mold, the overarching theme remains clear: flexibility, strategic planning, and alignment with personal values are key. By carefully tailoring your financial strategies to support your unique lifestyle choices, you can work toward a retirement designed to be not only financially sustainable but deeply rewarding. In the following segments, we'll explore tax planning, healthcare, and insurance considerations, further rounding out our guide to financial strategies for crafting a portfolio of passions in retirement.

Tax Planning and Legal Considerations

Navigating the complexities of tax obligations and legal requirements is a crucial aspect of financial planning. Whether you're living abroad, starting a new venture, or engaging in philanthropic activities, understanding and effectively managing your tax liabilities and legal obligations can significantly impact your financial health and peace of mind in retirement.

Tax-Efficient Withdrawal Strategies

A critical component of retirement planning is determining the most tax-efficient methods for withdrawing from your retirement accounts. I recommend working with a financial advisor to develop a withdrawal strategy that aims to minimize your tax liabilities while helping to ensure you have sufficient income for your needs. This strategy may involve tapping into taxable accounts first to take advantage of lower tax rates on long-term capital gains, followed by tax-deferred accounts like 401(k)s and IRAs.

Guiding Tip: Don't Get Caught Out

Watch out for the impact of Required Minimum Distributions (RMDs) on your tax situation. Planning for these mandatory withdrawals can help avoid unnecessary tax burdens.

International Tax Considerations

For retirees who choose to live abroad part of the year or embark on extended global travels, understanding the tax implications in both your home country and abroad is essential. Issues such as double taxation agreements, foreign earned income exclusions, and tax treaties can significantly affect your financial strategy.

> ### Guiding Tip: Get Help With Expat Taxes
>
> Expatriate taxes can be complex, but with the right planning and advice, you can navigate these waters more confidently lowering the risk of your retirement dreams being derailed by unforeseen tax complications.

It's crucial to consult with a tax professional experienced in international tax law to ensure compliance and optimize your tax situation across borders. Proper planning can prevent unexpected tax liabilities and help you take advantage of available tax benefits for expatriates and global travelers.

Legal Documentation and Estate Planning

Legal considerations, including estate planning, are vital components of a comprehensive retirement strategy. Ensuring that you have the necessary legal documents in place, such as wills, trusts, powers of attorney, and healthcare directives, can provide peace of mind and help ensure that your wishes are honored.

For those considering starting a non-profit or living abroad, additional legal considerations may come into play. Establishing the legal structure for a business, understanding international property laws, or navigating the legalities of philanthropic activities requires specialized legal advice.

I strongly advise working with legal professionals who have expertise in the specific areas relevant to your retirement goals. This collaboration can help ensure that your legal and financial strategies are aligned, providing a solid foundation for your retirement plans.

Guiding Tip: Consider a Living Trust – Cover Your Bases!

A comprehensive estate plan helps ensure your assets, values, and wishes are preserved and passed on according to your desires. This thoughtful planning can provide peace of mind and clarity for you and your loved ones.

The financial landscape of retirement is dotted with both opportunities and challenges. Effective tax planning and adherence to legal requirements are critical for navigating this landscape successfully. By proactively managing these aspects of your financial strategy, you can help mitigate potential pitfalls and ensure that your retirement journey is both fulfilling and financially sound.

As we progress, we'll turn our attention to planning for healthcare and insurance—key considerations that underpin the viability of any retirement lifestyle.

Planning for Healthcare and Insurance

The quest for a fulfilling retirement is intrinsically linked to our health and wellbeing. As such, planning for healthcare and securing the right insurance coverage are indispensable components of a comprehensive retirement strategy.

Medicare and Supplemental Insurance

For many retirees, Medicare serves as the foundation of their healthcare coverage. However, it's important to recognize that Medicare doesn't cover everything. Traditional Medicare includes Part A (hospital insurance) and Part B (medical insurance), but it often requires supplemental insurance, known as Medigap, to cover out-of-pocket expenses such as copayments, coinsurance, and deductibles. Additionally, Part D prescription drug plans can help manage medication costs. Understanding the various parts of Medicare and selecting the right supplemental plans can prevent unexpected medical expenses and provide peace of mind.

Long-Term Care Insurance

As we age, the likelihood of needing long-term care increases. Long-term care insurance can help cover the costs associated with assisted living, nursing homes, or in-home care, which are typically not covered by Medicare. It's crucial to consider purchasing long-term care insurance well before retirement, as premiums increase with age and health conditions. This type of insurance can protect your savings and ensure you receive the necessary care without burdening your family financially.

Healthcare Considerations for Frequent Travelers and Expats

Retirees who travel frequently or live abroad need to consider how their healthcare coverage aligns with their lifestyle. Traditional Medicare does not typically cover medical expenses incurred outside the United States. Therefore, it's advisable to look into international health insurance plans or travel insurance policies that provide comprehensive coverage during extended stays abroad. For those living abroad permanently, understanding the local healthcare system and securing adequate health insurance in the host country is essential.

Employer-Sponsored Retiree Health Plans

Some retirees may have access to employer-sponsored retiree health plans, which can be a valuable resource for managing healthcare costs. These plans often provide coverage that complements Medicare and may include additional benefits such as dental, vision, and prescription drug coverage. It's important to review the terms of these plans and understand how they integrate with Medicare to maximize your benefits.

Health Savings Accounts (HSAs)

For those who have been contributing to a Health Savings Account (HSA) while employed, these funds can be a valuable resource in retirement. HSAs offer triple tax advantages: contributions are generally tax-deductible (as long as the contributions do not exceed the annual contribution limits set by the IRS), growth is tax-free, and withdrawals for qualified medical expenses are also generally tax-free. Utilizing HSA funds for healthcare expenses in retirement can help reduce your out-of-pocket costs and support financial flexibility.

Preventive Care and Wellness

Planning for healthcare in retirement isn't solely about insurance; it's also about maintaining your health through preventive care and wellness practices. Regular check-ups, screenings, and vaccinations can help detect and prevent potential health issues. Additionally, adopting a healthy lifestyle that includes a balanced diet, regular exercise, and stress management techniques can improve your overall wellbeing and reduce healthcare costs in the long run.

Estate Planning and Healthcare Directives

As part of comprehensive healthcare planning, it's important to include healthcare directives in your estate planning. Documents such as a living will, durable power of attorney for healthcare, and do-not-resuscitate (DNR) orders ensure your medical wishes are respected if you become unable to communicate them yourself. Discussing these directives with your family and healthcare providers can provide clarity and prevent conflicts during difficult times.

Long-Term Sustainability

Ensure that your plans are sustainable in the long run. The key to longevity in any retirement plan lies in adaptability, proactive planning, and a clear understanding of the financial implications of your lifestyle choices.

> **Guiding Tip: Have Annual Checkups for Your Financial Plans**
>
> Embrace the principle of flexibility in your retirement planning. An annual financial "health check" can help ensure your retirement journey remains on course, even as your life and the world around you evolve.

I recommend scheduling annual financial reviews, either on your own or with a financial advisor. These reviews should encompass investment performance, spending patterns, and any changes in your retirement goals or lifestyle. This process helps to ensure that your financial strategy remains aligned with your aspirations and is responsive to the economic landscape.

Sustainability often hinges on how well you've diversified your income sources. Reliance on a single income stream can be risky, especially if your retirement path includes elements like entrepreneurship, which might have unpredictable income flows.

Exploring various income avenues, such as rental properties, dividends from investments, freelance work, or even creating online content, can provide financial stability and flexibility. Diversification not only helps in managing risks but also in capitalizing on opportunities for growth and expansion in your retirement endeavors.

An essential aspect of ensuring long-term sustainability is preparing for the unforeseen. Life can throw unexpected curveballs, and having a solid contingency plan, including a well-stocked emergency fund, is crucial.

I advise maintaining an emergency fund that can cover at least six months of living expenses. This fund can be a financial lifeline in times of need, offering protection against unforeseen expenses or income fluctuations without necessitating a dip into long-term investments or savings.

The Value of Working with a Financial Advisor

Navigating the complexities of retirement planning can be overwhelming, which is why working with a financial advisor can be so valuable. Advisors are required to complete hours of continuing education to stay updated on economic conditions, market trends, and emerging strategies. This ongoing education helps ensure they can provide informed and timely advice, helping you adjust your retirement strategy as needed.

Instead of trying to stay abreast of every financial development on your own, a financial advisor can bring expertise and a proactive approach, working to ensure your retirement plan remains viable and aligned with your evolving goals.

Moreover, be open to adjusting your lifestyle choices and goals as necessary. Flexibility and a willingness to adapt are your best allies in maintaining a sustainable, fulfilling retirement. This final segment of our exploration into crafting a retirement that breaks the mold focuses on harmonizing the practical aspects of financial stability with the emotional and psychological components of a satisfying retirement life.

The key to achieving this balance lies in recognizing that financial health is not an end in itself but a means to support and enrich your life's experiences. It's about creating a retirement that resonates with who you are, what you love, and how you envision your best life.

Guiding Tip: Navigate Newsletter

Financial stability in retirement is about more than just securing the resources you need to live; it's about unlocking the freedom to pursue the passions and purposes that infuse your life with meaning and joy. Subscribing to our "Navigate" financial newsletter can guide you toward achieving that freedom. Each issue offers valuable insights and practical tips that help you navigate the complexities of financial planning with confidence. Stay informed on the latest strategies and trends to help ensure your retirement funds your dreams to the fullest extent possible. Visit: www.EarlyStartRetirement.com to sign up!

Aligning Financial Well-Being with Personal Fulfillment

At the heart of a fulfilling retirement is the alignment between your financial well-being and your personal aspirations. This alignment ensures that your financial decisions support your lifestyle goals, whether that involves traveling the world, contributing to your community, or exploring new hobbies and interests.

I recommend starting this alignment process by clearly defining what fulfillment looks like for you. Revisit and update the notes you made at the start of the financial planning process. Think about the activities and experiences that give you joy, fulfillment, and meaning. Once you have a clear vision, you can tailor your financial planning to ensure it facilitates these aspirations, rather than constraining them.

A fulfilling retirement is also grounded in setting realistic expectations—both financially and in terms of what you aim to achieve. It's essential to approach retirement with an open mind and a willingness to find joy in both the grand adventures and the simple pleasures of everyday life.

Adjusting your expectations may mean redefining what success and happiness look like in retirement. For some, it could mean scaling down travel plans to explore more local destinations deeply. For others, it might involve finding fulfillment in volunteering and giving back to the community, rather than pursuing more costly endeavors.

Guiding Tip: Watching the Sunset with My Granddaughter, Isabel

True contentment in retirement is often found in the beauty of simple moments. Take, for instance, a serene evening I spent with my granddaughter, Isabel. She set up chairs and a picnic for us to watch the sunset, adding touches like toys for play and grapes for a snack—just in case. As the sun dipped behind the trees, our laughter and joy filled the air. It's these precious, unassuming experiences that truly enrich our lives and exemplify what we aim to cherish in retirement.

Ultimately, the richness of your retirement life is defined not by your financial wealth, but by the wealth of experiences, relationships, and personal growth you cultivate. Financial strategies and planning are essential tools that enable you to pursue the retirement you envision, but they are not the end goal. The true measure of a successful retirement is the joy, satisfaction, and sense of purpose you derive from how you choose to spend your time and resources.

In wrapping up our discussion on achieving a fulfilling and financially sound retirement, it's clear that the journey requires thoughtful planning, a proactive approach to managing finances, and a commitment to aligning those finances with your personal vision for retirement. By prioritizing flexibility, setting realistic expectations, and focusing on what truly brings you fulfillment, you can craft a retirement that's not only designed to be financially secure but also richly rewarding in every sense.

CHAPTER NINE

Overcoming Challenges & Navigating "Life Quakes" in Retirement

Embarking on retirement presents a multitude of challenges and changes, often accompanied by what I call "Life Quakes." This term, coined by Deb Delisi of the Abundant Love Project, describes the profound impact of events such as the loss of a spouse or receiving a diagnosis like cancer or Alzheimer's. These life-altering moments are not about overcoming or flourishing but about surviving and finding support during times of deep grief and loss.

This chapter will guide you through the tumultuous waters of retirement's uncertainties with grace and resilience. We'll explore how a strong financial plan can provide a safety net during these critical moments, allowing you to focus on your emotional well-being. You will learn strategies to manage financial stability amidst personal crises, so that your financial health can remain robust even when faced with significant life challenges.

Additionally, we'll discuss practical steps for preparing for potential "Life Quakes," from maintaining flexible and diversified income streams to understanding the importance of insurance and estate planning. By the end of this chapter, you'll be equipped with the knowledge and tools to navigate retirement's most difficult times, transforming obstacles into opportunities for support and stability.

> ### Guiding Tip: Starting Early to Overcome Challenges
>
> Starting your retirement planning early allows you to build a robust financial cushion, giving you more leeway to manage unexpected expenses or economic downturns. By taking proactive steps now, such as diversifying your investment portfolio or setting clear financial goals, you can navigate potential challenges with greater confidence and flexibility. Early planning also offers the advantage of time, which not only helps in compounding your savings but also in adjusting your strategies as circumstances change, thereby aiming for a smoother and potentially more secure retirement path.

Dealing with Uncertainty and Fear of the Unknown

Retirement, often envisioned as a time of relaxation and fulfillment, also brings its fair share of uncertainty and the unknown. As we transition from structured work lives to more open-ended days, the lack of routine can feel both liberating and unsettling. Embracing this uncertainty requires a mindset shift—seeing it not as a source of anxiety but as an opportunity for growth and exploration.

Guiding Tip: Embrace Uncertainty

Uncertainty is the soil in which opportunity grows. Water it with curiosity and watch new paths unfold. Harnessing *curiosity* in challenging situations can transform obstacles into opportunities for learning and growth, encouraging a deeper understanding and innovative solutions.

Beyond finances and health, emotional resilience plays a key role in dealing with uncertainty in retirement. Staying connected with a supportive community, whether through social groups, volunteer work, or family ties, helps anchor us during turbulent times. Embracing new hobbies, learning opportunities, and travel can also provide a sense of purpose and adventure, transforming the unknown from a source of fear into a canvas of possibilities. By preparing for uncertainty and maintaining a flexible, adaptive approach, we can navigate retirement with confidence and joy.

Life's only constant is change, and nowhere is this truer than in retirement. Staying adaptable means being open to altering your plans, exploring new directions, and pivoting when necessary. This flexibility is crucial in navigating the transitions retirement brings, allowing you to embrace life's ebbs and flows with grace and ease.

No one navigates retirement alone. Building a strong support network of family, friends, peers, and professionals can provide the encouragement and advice needed to overcome challenges. This network becomes a foundation of strength, offering diverse perspectives and support through every transition.

Communities, both physical and virtual, offer a wealth of resources for retirees facing transitions. From local clubs and online forums to professional services and educational workshops, these resources can provide guidance, companionship, and practical assistance on your journey.

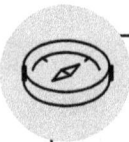

> ### Guiding Tip: Build a Support Network
> Surround yourself with a community that uplifts and supports you, and you'll find the strength to face any challenge.

Developing Coping Strategies and Resilience

The foundation of resilience in the face of retirement challenges often lies in our ability to stay grounded and maintain a positive outlook. Mindfulness practices, such as meditation or journaling, can offer solace and clarity, helping to navigate through times of uncertainty with a sense of calm. Similarly, fostering a positive outlook—choosing to see setbacks as temporary and surmountable—can significantly impact our emotional well-being and resilience.

Guiding Tip: Author Gregg Braden on Resilience

Gregg Braden, influential thought leader on resilience, believes that "the key to our transformation is simply this: the better we know ourselves the better equipped we will be to make our choices wisely."

This perspective emphasizes the importance of self-awareness and understanding as foundational elements of resilience, particularly during challenging times.

Building emotional resilience is akin to strengthening a muscle; it requires consistent effort and the right exercises. Techniques such as setting small, achievable goals, practicing gratitude, and engaging in activities that bring joy can enhance your emotional resilience. These practices don't just help in overcoming current challenges but also in preparing for future ones, making you more robust and adaptable.

Embracing Lifelong Learning and Skill Development

Adopting a lifelong learning mindset is essential for overcoming the various challenges that retirement can bring. Engaging in continuous education, whether through formal classes, online courses, or self-directed learning, not only keeps the mind sharp but also fosters neuroplasticity, literally creating new neural pathways that enhance cognitive resilience. This cognitive engagement can significantly reduce the risk of mental decline, making lifelong learning a powerful tool for maintaining mental health during retirement.

The benefits of lifelong learning extend beyond cognitive health. Acquiring new skills and knowledge can open doors to a myriad of opportunities. For instance, learning a new language or acquiring technical skills can make travel more enriching, enable you to volunteer in new capacities, or even embark on a second career that aligns with your passions. According to research from the National Institute on Aging, staying intellectually engaged can also improve overall life satisfaction and emotional well-being.

Furthermore, the process of learning itself instills valuable life skills such as adaptability, resilience, and a growth mindset. These skills are particularly relevant in retirement, a phase often marked by significant transitions and changes. Lifelong learning encourages you to embrace new challenges, adapt to unexpected situations, and remain open to new experiences. As noted by the American Psychological Association, a commitment to learning can help you develop the flexibility needed to navigate the uncertainties of retirement.

Incorporating lifelong learning into your retirement plan can thus serve as a compass, guiding you through the unfamiliar territories of this new life stage. By continually seeking out new knowledge and skills, you can ensure that your retirement years are not only fulfilling but also dynamic and resilient. This approach helps you stay engaged with the world around you, fostering a sense of purpose and ongoing personal growth.

Building a Supportive Network and Seeking Guidance

As we traverse the landscape of retirement, guidance from those who have walked the path before us can be invaluable. Seeking mentors, whether in personal or professional capacities, can provide insights, encouragement, and practical advice to help navigate the complexities of retirement. These relationships enrich our journey, offering perspectives and wisdom gleaned from experience.

For many aspects of retirement planning, especially those involving financial, legal, or health considerations, professional advice is not just helpful; it's essential. Financial advisors, legal experts, and healthcare professionals can offer guidance tailored to your unique situation, ensuring that your plans are robust, comprehensive, and aligned with your goals.

In navigating the challenges and transitions inherent in retirement our resilience, adaptability, and willingness to learn and seek guidance form the bedrock of a fulfilling journey. As we look ahead, embracing these strategies not only prepares us for the roadblocks but also enhances the richness of our retirement experience, turning potential obstacles into opportunities for growth and joy.

Utilizing Resources and Tools for Transitions

The landscape of retirement is dotted with resources designed to ease the journey through its transitions. From digital platforms offering courses on financial literacy to communities that provide emotional support, the tools at your disposal are both varied and valuable.

Online platforms and apps present a treasure trove of information and support for retirees. Whether it's managing investments, learning new skills, or simply connecting with like-minded individuals, the digital realm offers endless possibilities. I recommend identifying tools that not only provide valuable information but also encourage interaction and engagement, creating a sense of community even in virtual spaces.

Many organizations and institutions offer workshops and seminars specifically tailored to retirees. These sessions can cover a range of topics, from health and wellness to estate planning and digital literacy. Participating in these events provides not just knowledge but also the opportunity to engage with peers, sharing experiences and advice.

Mindset Shifts and Positive Psychology

At the heart of navigating retirement's transitions successfully is the belief in one's ability to grow and adapt. This growth mindset encourages curiosity, resilience, and openness to new experiences, traits that are invaluable as you chart your course through retirement.

Incorporating elements of positive psychology—such as focusing on strengths, practicing gratitude, and seeking moments of joy—can significantly impact your well-being and satisfaction in retirement. It's about shifting the focus from what's lacking to what's abundant, from what's lost to what's gained.

> ### Guiding Tip: Cultivate Your Mindset
> Your mindset shapes your retirement journey. Cultivate one that sees every day as an opportunity for growth, joy, and discovery.

Celebrating Triumphs and Lessons Learned

Retirement is a mosaic of experiences—some challenging, some exhilarating. Recognizing and celebrating each triumph, no matter how small, is crucial. It reinforces your sense of accomplishment and propels you forward with renewed enthusiasm.

Take time to reflect on your journey, acknowledging the progress you've made and the obstacles you've overcome. Celebrate these milestones, whether they're related to personal goals, financial achievements, or simply the successful navigation of a difficult transition.

Equally important is the ability to extract lessons from every experience. Viewing setbacks not as failures but as learning opportunities enriches your retirement journey, equipping you with wisdom and insight for future challenges.

By leveraging the myriad resources available, embracing a mindset of growth and positivity, and celebrating every step of the journey, retirees can navigate the complexities of this life stage with grace and fulfillment, making the most of the opportunities it presents for personal evolution and joy.

Every triumph and lesson contribute to the richness of your story. Celebrate them all, for they are invaluable to your journey.

Dealing with a "Life Quake" - The Loss of a Spouse

Losing a spouse is one of the most profound life quakes one can experience, bringing immense emotional and practical challenges. This section offers strategies to navigate this difficult period, providing both immediate and long-term guidance to help you through the grief and adjustments that follow such a significant loss.

Immediate Steps Following the Loss

Allow Yourself to Grieve: Acknowledging and expressing your emotions is crucial. Grief is a natural response to loss, and it's essential to allow yourself the space to feel and process these emotions. Seek support from family, friends, or a professional therapist who can provide a safe space to talk about your feelings and experiences.

Avoid Major Life Changes: During the first year after your spouse's death, it's advisable to avoid making any significant decisions, such as moving to a new home or selling property. This period is about maintaining stability and allowing yourself time to adjust. Keeping things as consistent as possible can help you find your footing before making any substantial changes.

Practical Tips for Managing Financial and Legal Matters

Bank Accounts and Financial Management: Initially, keep your spouse's name on checking accounts and other financial documents. This can prevent complications and provide time to organize your finances.

Arrange a Meeting with a Financial Advisor: They can help you review your accounts, update beneficiaries, and develop a clear financial plan moving forward. Your financial advisor can be an invaluable asset during this time, as they are typically well-versed in handling these types of situations. They can provide guidance on managing your current finances, ensuring that all necessary updates are made, and help you navigate any immediate financial concerns. Additionally, they can assist in planning for your future financial stability, addressing any long-term financial goals you may have, and offering support as you adjust to your new circumstances.

Dealing with Insurance and Benefits: Notify insurance companies about your spouse's passing and understand your benefits entitlements. This might include life insurance payouts and Social Security survivor benefits. Apply for these benefits promptly to ensure you receive the financial support you're entitled to.

Estate Planning and Legal Documentation: Review and update your wills, trusts, and power of attorney documents. Consulting with an attorney can ensure that all legal documents are current and reflect your new circumstances. This step is crucial for helping to secure your financial future and making sure your wishes are legally documented.

Emotional and Psychological Strategies

Establish a Support System: Connecting with family, friends, and support groups is vital. They can provide emotional support and practical help during this time. Consider joining grief counseling or therapy groups where you can share your experiences with others who understand what you're going through.

Create a Routine: Developing a daily routine can provide structure and normalcy. Incorporate self-care activities such as exercise, hobbies, and mindfulness practices into your routine.

These activities can offer comfort and a sense of stability as you navigate your grief.

Allow Yourself Time to Heal: Understand that grief is a process and give yourself time to adjust. Be patient and compassionate with yourself, recognizing that healing takes time. There's no right or wrong way to grieve, and it's important to honor your own journey.

Long-term Considerations

Financial Planning and Stability: Regularly review your financial plans with a financial advisor to help maintain ongoing financial security. Planning for future needs, such as healthcare and living expenses, can provide peace of mind and stability.

Reconnecting with Personal Goals and Passions: As you move forward, reconnect with hobbies and interests that bring joy and fulfillment. Consider volunteering or engaging in community activities to foster a sense of purpose. These activities can provide a positive focus and help you rebuild your life.

Taking small, manageable steps during this difficult time is crucial. Seek support, stay connected with loved ones, and be proactive about addressing both emotional and practical challenges. A strong financial plan and a compassionate approach to your own healing process can help you navigate the complexities of losing a spouse, ensuring you find stability and support as you move forward.

• •▶

Key Takeaways

- **Strong Financial Planning:** Establishing a solid financial foundation is crucial for navigating the uncertainties and "Life Quakes" in retirement. This includes early and ongoing planning to build a robust financial cushion.

- **Dealing with Uncertainty:** Embrace the unknown as an opportunity for growth. Staying flexible and adaptable helps manage the lack of routine and unexpected changes in retirement.

- **Support Networks:** Building and maintaining a strong support network of family, friends, and professionals provides emotional and practical support during challenging times.

- **Lifelong Learning:** Adopting a lifelong learning mindset enhances adaptability and resilience. Continuous education keeps the mind sharp and opens up new possibilities for personal growth and engagement.

- **Coping Strategies:** Developing emotional resilience through mindfulness practices, setting small goals, and maintaining a positive outlook can help navigate the transitions and challenges of retirement.

- **Dealing with Loss:** In the face of profound losses like the death of a spouse, practical steps and emotional support are essential. Avoid major life changes initially, seek professional financial advice, and allow yourself time to heal.

These strategies collectively help in transforming retirement challenges into opportunities for growth and fulfillment, ensuring a supportive and resilient journey through this life stage.

CHAPTER TEN

Crafting Your Personalized Retirement Plan

P lanning for retirement is akin to preparing for a grand adventure or embarking on the creation of a masterful piece of art. It's a process that demands introspection, creativity, and a willingness to explore the uncharted territories of one's future. Let me be your guide through this exciting period, offering insights and strategies to help you mold a retirement experience that mirrors your deepest values, passions, and aspirations. Here, we will lay the foundation for a retirement plan that is as dynamic and vibrant as life itself, one that evolves alongside you, accommodating changes and embracing new possibilities with open arms.

Guiding Tip: Crafting Your Unique Early Start Retirement Plan

As you embark on crafting your unique Early Start Retirement Plan, envision it as creating a diverse portfolio of passions that enriches your life today and continues to do so in the years to come. This journey is about more than just financial planning; it's about identifying and cultivating the activities and interests that bring you joy, satisfaction, and a sense of purpose. By thoughtfully integrating these elements into your retirement strategy, you can ensure a fulfilling and dynamic retirement that resonates with your aspirations and values.

Preliminaries: Your Financial Situation

First, assess your expected financial situation during mini-retirements and after your formal retirement (see Chapter 8, Financial Strategies for Early Start Retirement Plans). Your financial resources will largely dictate what you can achieve. Once you have identified your passions, goals, and desired activities for retirement, you may need to revisit and adjust your financial plan. Your financial strategy and desired activities are closely connected, ensuring that both align to support a fulfilling retirement. See, "Example: Sarah's Retirement Planning, Financial Foundation," in the following section.

Unearthing Your Core Values, Passions, and Goals

The cornerstone of a fulfilling retirement plan lies in deep introspection and understanding of what truly matters to you. This is a time to dig into the essence of your being, to uncover the values, passions, and goals that will shape your retirement into a period of life that is not just meaningful but deeply rewarding.

Start with a period of self-reflection. This is an exercise designed to peel back the layers of your life's experiences, helping you to identify the moments of highest satisfaction, purpose, and joy. This exploration is the first step in aligning your retirement plan with the core of who you are.

Guiding Tip: Discovering What Makes You Thrive

Reflect on your life's most enriching moments to illuminate the path toward a retirement filled with purpose and passion.

Example: Sarah's Retirement Planning, Financial Foundation

Sarah Jones: Persona and Sample Information Sheet

Sarah Jones is an imaginary person, a 45-year-old physical

therapist living in Seattle, Washington. She is married with two children and enjoys an active lifetsyle, including hiking and traveling.

Desired Retirement Age: 62

Current Income and Savings:

- Annual Salary: $100,000
- Retirement Savings: $300,00 (includes 401(k) and IRA)
- Expected Retirement Expenses: Sarah estimates needing $60,000 per year in retirement to maintain her current lifestyle. This includes adjusting for inflation.

Debt:

- Sarah has a mortgage of $200,000 remaining with a monthly payment of $1,500. She expects to pay this off in 15 years.

Risk Tolerance:

- Sarah is moderately comfortable with investing in the stock market. She understands the potential of higher returns comes with the possibility of larger losses.

Additional Notes:

- Sarah's employer offers a 401(k) with a 4% company match.
- Sarah is eligible or Social Security benefits, but the exact amount is unknown at this time.

This information sheet provides a starting point for Sarah's retirement plan. By considering these factors, we can develop a personalized strategy to help her achieve her retirement goals.

• ▶

From Passions to Goals

Once you have listed and reviewed your values and passions the next step is to turn them into a set of retirement goals. But note that retirement planning is not about setting a course in stone; it's about sketching out a roadmap that can adapt and change as you do. Flexibility and adaptability are your allies, ensuring that your retirement plan remains relevant and responsive to life's inevitable shifts and turns.

Your retirement plan as a living document, one that you revisit and revise as circumstances evolve. It's a blueprint for the future that respects the fluid nature of life.

In the example ahead, you can see Sarah's lists of values, passions, and goals.

Example: Sarah's Retirement Planning, Values, Passions, and Goals

Core Values:

- Adventure
- Creativity
- Financial Security
- Lifelong Learning
- Making a Difference

Passions:

- Spending Time with family and friends
- Learning to play the piano

- Volunteering with environmental causes
- Starting a vegetable garden
- Writing a novel
- Travelling

Retirement Goals:
- Learn Spanish
- Hike the Inca Trail in Peru by age 65
- Take a pottery class and sell creations at local markets within 2 years.
- Spend 20 hours a month volunteering at a homeless shelter.
- Gain self-sufficiency by growing 50% of my own veggies
- Finish writing and publish a historical fiction novel.

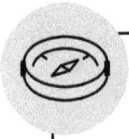

Guiding Tip: Crafting a Flexible Future
Your retirement plan as a dynamic guide, capable of evolving with you through the twists and turns of life.

Action and Adaptability: The Dynamic Duo of Retirement Planning

With your core values and passions providing a roadmap, you can start to identify your retirement goals. This is where your vision begins to take shape, transforming from ideas into reality.

It's helpful to visualize your dream retirement, and creating a vision board is a fantastic starting point. This collage of images, words, and quotes can capture anything from relaxing on a beach to volunteering abroad. With a vivid picture in mind, you can transform those dreams into concrete goals by applying a reimagined SMART goals framework. In this context, SMART stands for:

Spectacular: Your goals should be inspiring and exciting.

Memorable: They should be meaningful enough to stay in your mind.

Amazing: Aim for goals that truly enhance your sense of wonder and fulfillment.

Rewarding: Ensure each goal brings a sense of achievement and satisfaction.

Time Allocated: Dedicate specific time frames to accomplish these goals.

This framework offers a dynamic structure for setting goals that are not just practical but also deeply enriching. For instance, Sarah might set a goal to "become conversationally fluent in Spanish and volunteer at a Costa Rican animal shelter, dedicating the next five years to achieving this amazing and rewarding journey."

The following table shows how Sarah divided her retired life into chapters and organized her goals so that generally the most vigorous activities would be enjoyed while she was most active, and the most sedate activities were scheduled for a time when she might be less inclined to climb mountains.

Example: Sarah's Retirement Planning, Activities for Life Chapters

Retirement Age	Life Chapter	Goals	Activities
Early (55-65)	Travel and Exploration	Hike the Inca Trail, learn Spanish, self-sufficiency	Backpacking trips, language courses, volunteer work in Latin America, Grow vegetables
Middle (65-75)	Creativity & Community	Take pottery classes, sell creations	Local art classes, farmers markets, volunteer teaching pottery to children
Later (75+)	Purpose & Legacy	Volunteer at homeless shelter, write a novel	Volunteer shifts, writing workshops, joining a writers' group

. . . . ▶

Exercise: Consider Maximizing Potential with Shorter Planning Cycles

Consider the benefits of designing your life in smaller, manageable segments, such as 3-5 year chunks. This approach aligns with the natural rhythms and transitions we experience, allowing for more frequent reassessments and adjustments. By breaking your long-term goals into shorter periods, you can ensure your plans stay relevant and responsive to changes in your personal circumstances and aspirations. This method helps transform overwhelming goals into more achievable, engaging tasks.

Reflect on incorporating this strategy into your retirement planning. For example, you might dedicate the first few years to learning a new skill or hobby, followed by a period focused on travel or volunteering. How could this keep your retirement dynamic and engaging? Think about structuring your retirement as a series of exciting chapters, each with its own set of goals and activities. This exercise aims to foster a fulfilling retirement while also encouraging adaptability and personal growth over time.

Realigning with Financial Plans

Now is a good time to revisit your financial plan and ensure that it is still in sync with your action plan. As time passes, Sarah will no doubt change some goals and activities, and firm up others. It's a good idea to make a more formal review at regular intervals—perhaps every year on the anniversary of your first retirement plan.

A Checklist for Crafting Your Dream Retirement, Step-by-Step

Step 1: Unearthing Your Compass - Core Values and Passions

- Self-discovery: Ask yourself, "What truly matters to me?" Identify your core values, the guiding principles that shape your life. Do you value adventure, creativity, financial security, or making a difference?

- Passion ignites: Reflect on your passions. What activities bring you joy and a sense of fulfillment? Is it creating art, traveling the world, nurturing a garden?

Step 2: Charting Your Course - Goals and Objectives

- Vision board: Create a vision board for your ideal retirement. Include images, words, or quotes that represent your desired lifestyle.
- SMART Goals: Set Spectacular, Meaningful, Amazing, Rewarding, and Time-Allocated goals. For example, "Learn Spanish and volunteer at a local animal shelter in Costa Rica within the next five years."

Step 3: Mapping Your Terrain - Activities and Timeline

- Life chapters: Divide your retirement into different chapters. Early retirement might be focused on travel, while a later chapter could involve pursuing a creative passion.
- Activity matrix: Create a table with your retirement goals and activities listed on one axis and your life chapters on the other. Fill in the table with how you'll achieve those goals through specific activities in each chapter.

Step 4: Financial Navigation, Aligning Income and Savings

- Estimate needs: Research and estimate your expected expenses in retirement. Consider factors like healthcare costs, desired lifestyle, and travel plans.

- Income streams: Identify your retirement income sources – Social Security, pensions, investment income, etc.
- Savings gap: Calculate the difference between your estimated expenses and projected income. This will determine how much you need to save.
- Investment strategy: Develop an investment strategy to bridge the savings gap. Consider your risk tolerance and time horizon.

Step 5: Embracing Flexibility—Your Dynamic Plan

- Life is a journey: Your retirement plan is a living document, not set in stone. Revisit and adjust your plan as your priorities and circumstances change.
- Embrace the unexpected: Leave room for serendipity. Unexpected opportunities might lead you down exciting new paths.

Remember:

- Multiple options: I encourage a multifaceted approach. You can combine different options like part-time work, volunteer work, and pursuing hobbies.
- Flexibility is key: Your plan should allow you to adapt to changing situations, health needs, and financial realities.
- Enjoy the journey: Creating your retirement plan is an exciting process. Let it spark your imagination and fuel your enthusiasm for the adventures that await!

> ### Guiding Tip: Making Dreams Reality
>
> The leap from planning to action is bridged by courage and adaptability. Embrace them and watch your retirement dreams unfold.

From Plan to Action

Moving from planning to action is often where challenges arise. Fear, procrastination, and resistance to change can stymie even the most well-thought-out retirement plans. Larger goals can seem overwhelming. Break them down into smaller, more manageable tasks, making the path to achievement clear and less daunting.

Break your actions into manageable steps to combat procrastination. Address fears directly by identifying worst-case scenarios and planning for them, reducing the fear of the unknown. Change is inevitable. Embracing it requires a mindset shift—seeing change as an opportunity for growth and enrichment rather than a threat. Taking the first step might be daunting, but every journey begins with just that—a single step, followed by another, and then another.

In crafting your personalized retirement plan, you're not merely plotting a course for the future; you're sculpting a life phase that resonates with vibrancy, growth, and fulfillment. Through introspection, adaptable planning, decisive action, and strategic goal setting, you lay the groundwork for a retirement that reflects not only who you are but who you aspire to be.

Balancing the immediate pleasures with long-term aspirations is critical in retirement planning. This balance ensures that short-term actions contribute to the realization of your overarching vision for retirement. Regular reflection on how daily activities align with long-term goals can help maintain this balance. It's about ensuring that today's choices don't detract from tomorrow's dreams. Consistency in actions and decisions, aligned with both short-term desires and long-term goals, is key to achieving a cohesive and fulfilling retirement.

Incorporating Risk-Taking & Exploration

The concept of risk-taking doesn't necessarily conjure images of financial gambles but rather the embrace of new experiences and the willingness to step beyond comfort zones. In retirement, this might mean relocating to a new country, diving into a hobby that's always intrigued you, or even starting a business related to a lifelong passion.

Embrace new ventures with openness. Retirement is the perfect stage of life for exploration. It's a time when the constraints of a 9-to-5 job no longer hold sway, offering the freedom to pursue interests that were previously sidelined. Encourage yourself to view each new venture as a learning opportunity, a chance to add depth and richness to your life.

The Role of Calculated Risks

Calculated risks, taken after careful consideration and planning, can lead to some of the most fulfilling experiences in retirement. Whether it's financial investment in a dream project or the personal investment of time in learning a new skill, each risk carries potential for growth and satisfaction.

Guiding Tip: The Thrill of Discovery

Retirement is your horizon of opportunity. Dare to venture beyond, and you'll discover treasures of experience and joy you never anticipated.

Celebrating Milestones Enhances Retirement Journeys

One of the most vital, yet often overlooked, aspects of navigating retirement is taking the time to acknowledge your progress and the milestones you've achieved. This celebration of progress not only reinforces a sense of accomplishment but also bolsters motivation for future endeavors. Setting aside moments to celebrate milestones, no matter how small, is crucial.

These markers of progress serve as reminders of your capabilities and the steps you've taken towards realizing your retirement dreams. They're beacons of achievement that light your path forward. Incorporate reflective practices into your routine, such as journaling or meditation, to ponder the experiences and lessons learned throughout your retirement journey. This reflection deepens your understanding of your growth and aids in steering your path forward with intention and insight.

Guiding Tip: Cherishing Each Step

Every milestone in your retirement journey is a testament to your growth and courage. Celebrate these achievements, for they are the milestones of a life richly lived.

Navigating the Balance Between Planning and Living

As you carve out your retirement plan, remember that the essence of retirement lies in the balance between meticulous planning and the spontaneity of living. It's about crafting a framework for your aspirations while remaining open to the unexpected joys and challenges that life unfurls.

Your retirement plan should serve as a flexible framework rather than a rigid itinerary. It's a guide that keeps you aligned with your goals and values while allowing room for the spontaneous and unforeseen. Embrace the fluidity of retirement, adjusting your sails as the winds of life shift.

While forward planning is crucial, equally important is

the ability to live in the moment—savoring the present, the everyday joys, and the beauty of the now. This balance between future aspirations and present experiences is the heart of a fulfilling retirement.

Guiding Tip: The Art of Balance

Retirement planning is the art of charting your future without losing sight of the value of the present. Find joy in the journey, not just the destination.

In crafting your personalized retirement plan, you're doing more than setting goals and making plans; you're designing a life stage rich with potential for growth, discovery, and fulfillment. Through embracing change, taking calculated risks, and celebrating your journey, you transform the concept of retirement from a time of winding down to a dynamic period of expansion and exploration.

Guiding Tip: Have the Courage to Discover

Dare to explore beyond the familiar. Your retirement is the perfect chapter for new experiences and personal growth.

In summary, retirement planning is not about setting a course in stone; it's about sketching out a roadmap that can adapt and change as you go. Flexibility and adaptability are your allies, ensuring that your retirement plan remains relevant and responsive to life's inevitable shifts and turns. Embrace the winds of change. Step outside your comfort zone. Enjoy the benefits of Your Early Start Retirement.

CHAPTER ELEVEN

Embracing the Freedom of Choice in Retirement

C rafting a retirement plan that truly reflects personal values, aspirations, and the freedom to choose one's own path is not just empowering—it's essential for a fulfilling post-career life. This chapter is a testament to the journey you've embarked upon through this book, embracing the myriad possibilities that retirement offers beyond traditional expectations. It's about recognizing that retirement is not a one-size-fits-all phase of life but a personal canvas awaiting your unique brushstrokes.

The Celebration of Choice

Retirement represents a significant shift from structured work life to a more fluid and self-directed phase. This transition offers an unparalleled opportunity to reflect on what truly matters to you. The power of choice in retirement is profound, offering the freedom to reshape your life around your deepest values and passions.

Whether it's pursuing hobbies long set aside, traveling to places you've dreamed of, or dedicating time to causes that move you, this phase of life opens up a spectrum of possibilities previously constrained by time or obligations.

Reflecting on the journey thus far, it's clear that the paths to fulfillment in retirement are as diverse as the individuals walking them. The stories shared in this book illustrate the benefits of embracing such freedom. They serve not just as inspiration but as a call to action—to view retirement as a realm of possibilities where the only limit is your imagination.

Recognizing the vast array of choices available can be both exhilarating and overwhelming. It's important to remember that each decision you make in retirement is an opportunity to tailor your life to your unique desires and circumstances. The choices you make can lead to new adventures, deeper relationships, and a richer, more fulfilling life.

As you navigate this new chapter, embrace the power of choice. Let it guide you to create a retirement that aims to be not only financially secure but also deeply satisfying and aligned with your passions. The freedom to choose is a powerful tool in crafting the life you've always envisioned.

Voices of Inspiration

The heart of this book lies in the powerful stories of those who've boldly chosen a portfolio of passions pre- and post-retirement. These narratives are as varied as they are inspiring, reflecting the myriad ways in which retirees today are redefining what it means to retire. It's evident that fulfillment in retirement transcends financial planning—it's deeply intertwined with personal growth, community connection, and the pursuit of joy.

Guiding Tip: A New Beginning

Let the stories of those who've walked before you light your path. Their journeys, with all their challenges and triumphs, remind us that retirement is not just an end but a beginning—a chance to rediscover and reinvent oneself.

Cultivating a Positive Outlook

Armed with the insights and strategies discussed throughout this book, you're now equipped with a deeper understanding of the vast array of retirement options available to you. The key is to approach this next phase of life with a positive and empowered perspective, recognizing that you have the tools and knowledge to design a retirement that aligns with your deepest desires.

Remember, the foundation of a fulfilling retirement lies in the choices you make—choices that reflect your values, aspirations, and the lifestyle you envision for yourself. It's about embracing the freedom to mold your retirement into a reflection of who you are and what you love.

Implementing New Strategies & Approaches

As you stand on the threshold of this new chapter, the importance of taking action cannot be overstated. Drawing on the lessons and strategies explored in this book, to begin laying the groundwork for your unique retirement journey, whether it's exploring new hobbies, planning your dream travel, or launching a venture that sparks your passion, the time to start is now.

Practical advice for embarking on this journey includes setting clear, achievable goals, creating a step-by-step plan for pursuing your interests, and seeking out communities or resources that support your chosen path. Remember, the journey of a thousand miles begins with a single step.

Embracing Change and Creating a Unique Retirement Journey

Viewing retirement as a dynamic and evolving journey means staying open to the unexpected and finding joy in the new and unknown. Embrace change not as a barrier but as a doorway to new experiences and deeper understandings of yourself and the world around you.

Curiosity plays a vital role in maintaining a sense of purpose and satisfaction throughout retirement. Staying curious about the world, new experiences, and even the challenges you face can transform your retirement into a period of ongoing growth and discovery. I am super excited about the concept of curiosity and how I use it to navigate both fun and challenging situations.

Curiosity encourages us to explore new hobbies, meet new people, and learn new skills. It helps us to see mistakes not as failures but as learning opportunities. This mindset is incredibly empowering, as it allows us to approach life with a sense of adventure and possibility. There are no mistakes, only learning opportunities, and each experience adds to the richness of our lives.

Adopting a lifelong learning mindset can help you overcome challenges you might face in retirement. Engaging in continuous education, whether through formal classes, online courses, or self-directed learning, keeps the mind sharp, opens up new possibilities, and enhances adaptability.

The skills and knowledge we acquire through lifelong learning can be powerful tools in navigating retirement's transitions. They can open doors to new hobbies, volunteer opportunities, or even second careers. Moreover, the process of learning itself—stepping into the unknown and mastering new domains—mirrors the broader journey of retirement, teaching us to embrace change with confidence.

Curiosity, combined with the freedom to choose how we spend our time, creates a powerful framework for a fulfilling and enriching retirement. By staying curious, being open to new experiences, and cultivating a mindset that sees change as an opportunity rather than a threat, we can ensure that our retirement years are not just a time in our life but a space for living life to its fullest.

Moving Forward with Confidence

As you step into the realm of retirement, armed with a wealth of knowledge and a heart full of aspirations, remember that confidence is key. Confidence not just in your ability to plan, but in your capacity to live out your retirement dreams in vibrant color. This confidence is bolstered by the realization that retirement offers a unique opportunity to design a life that reflects your true self, free from the constraints and expectations that may have previously held sway.

A New Chapter Begins

As we close this book, consider this not as an ending but as the commencement of the most exciting chapter yet. You stand at the threshold of a period in your life ripe with potential, armed with new perspectives and strategies to embark on a retirement journey uniquely yours. It's a chapter that promises growth, joy, adventure, and the deep satisfaction that comes from living in alignment with your true self.

Moving forward, let excitement and anticipation light your way. Embrace the wealth of possibilities that retirement holds, knowing that you possess the tools, insights, and courage to shape this chapter into one of the most fulfilling of your life. Remember, this is your journey, one that is as boundless and unique as you dare to make it.

> ### Guiding Tip: Write Your Masterpiece
> The next chapter of your life is a blank page, inviting you to craft a portfolio of passions and write your masterpiece. With pen in hand and a world of possibilities ahead, seize the opportunity to dream big and create a life filled with purpose and fulfillment.

Crafting Your Retirement Vision

Embracing the freedom of choice in retirement is about more than just how you spend your time; it's about how you live your life. It's a testament to the power of personal agency, the beauty of diversity in life's paths, and the enduring capacity for growth and fulfillment at any age. As you venture forth, remember that your retirement is your masterpiece, a work of art that you have the freedom and power to create. It's a reflection of your life's journey, your values, and your dreams.

Let this book serve as a guide, but let your heart and intuition be your true compass. You are equipped, inspired, and ready to embrace the myriad choices that lie before you with grace, enthusiasm, and anticipation. Here's to your retirement—a beautiful, ever-evolving masterpiece that is as unique and remarkable as you are.

Continuing Your Journey & Sharing Inspiration

As you embark on this exciting journey of crafting your

retirement, I invite you to visit our dedicated resource center at www.EarlyStartRetirement.com. Here, you'll find a wealth of additional tools, worksheets, and exclusive content designed to complement the insights and strategies discussed in this book.

The resource center is continually updated with new materials to help you implement the concepts tailored to your unique vision for retirement. By taking advantage of these resources, you can be confident that your planning process is both thorough and enjoyable, setting the stage for a vibrant and fulfilling retirement.

I sincerely hope you have found value in this book and that it has inspired you to dream big and plan a retirement that reflects your passions and aspirations. If you have, please consider sharing this book with someone you care about who might also benefit from its insights. Additionally, your feedback is incredibly important to me. If you could take a moment to write a review on Amazon, it would mean the world to me. Your thoughts not only help others discover this book but also support my mission to guide more people toward a fulfilling and purposeful retirement.

Thank you for joining me on this journey. Your future is bright, and I'm excited to see the masterpiece you create.

With every choice you make, every path you explore, and every new day you greet, know that you are crafting a legacy of wisdom, joy, and fulfillment—a true celebration of a life well-lived. May your retirement journey be everything you've envisioned and more. Here's to the beginning of your greatest adventure yet:

The Early Start Retirement Plan: Craft a Portfolio of Passions to Enrich Your Life Today and Beyond.

Page XIX

Did you know that people often spend more time planning their summer vacation than they do their retirement? It's a startling statistic that underscores a common oversight:

- AARP Study (2015): A survey by AARP found that 52% of Americans spend five hours or fewer planning for their financial future, while the average American spends about 10 hours planning a vacation.
- Charles Schwab Study (2019): According to a study by Charles Schwab, Americans spend approximately twice as much time planning their vacations (five hours) as they do on their 401(k) retirement plans (two hours).
- Northwestern Mutual Planning & Progress Study (2018): This study indicated that Americans spend an average of 10 hours planning a vacation but only about four hours planning their finances.
- Prudential Financial Study (2017): This study showed that 30% of Americans spend more time planning vacations than they do retirement.

Even more surprising, a recent study found that 42% of Americans just guess and stop working without a concrete plan:

- A study by Allianz Life conducted in 2023 revealed that a significant portion of Americans are uncertain about their retirement readiness. Specifically, the study found that 42% of Americans do not have a formal financial plan and often guess if they have enough to retire. Many do not even create a budget for their retirement years, highlighting a considerable gap in financial planning practices (Allianz Life).

Page 1

Research overwhelmingly points towards the benefits of staying active in retirement. Studies show that retirees who remain physically and mentally active have a lower risk of chronic diseases such as dementia, heart disease—and they enjoy a higher quality of life, greater happiness, and a more positive outlook.

- National Institute on Aging: Research shows that older adults who maintain an active lifestyle are less likely to develop chronic diseases such as dementia, heart disease, stroke, and some cancers. They also tend to have a longer lifespan, higher happiness levels, and greater resilience, which contributes to a more positive outlook on life (National Institute on Aging) (National Institute on Aging).

- Mayo Clinic: Regular exercise has been linked to a lower risk of dementia and improved cognitive function. It also helps reduce the risk of heart disease, control weight, and improve overall mood, contributing to better mental health and quality of life (Mayo Clinic).

- American Heart Association: Staying active helps delay or prevent chronic illnesses associated with aging, like heart disease and stroke. It also improves overall well-being, boosts mood, and promotes a positive attitude, which is crucial for maintaining a high quality of life in retirement (www.heart.org).

- Michigan State University Extension: Regular physical activity, such as walking, lowers the risk of developing dementia and other chronic diseases. It also improves mental focus, memory, and problem-solving skills, which are essential for maintaining mental health in older adults (AgriNat).

Page 56

There are more than 400,000 Americans living and working in the Philippines, including many active and retired US service personnel.

- According to the U.S. Embassy in the Philippines, there is a significant presence of U.S. citizens in the country, many of whom are retired military personnel taking advantage of the country's favorable retirement visa options (US Embassy).

- Moreover, the guide from Wise on moving to the Philippines notes that the country is a popular destination for expatriates, including a substantial number of Americans who are either working or retired there (Wise).

Page 109

Many countries offer digital nomad visas, which allow remote workers to live and work in the country for a temporary period; usually up to six-months or a year. At the time of writing there were about eight such destinations in each of Central-and-South America, the Caribbean, and Asia; and more than twenty in Europe.

- Central and South America: Countries like Costa Rica, Mexico, Belize, and Panama offer digital nomad visas. For example, Costa Rica's visa allows remote workers to stay for a year, extendable for another year, with a minimum income requirement of $3,000 per month (Citizen Remote).

- The Caribbean: The Bahamas, Barbados, and Saint Lucia are among the Caribbean nations with digital nomad visas. The Bahamas Extended Access Travel Stay (BEATS) program allows stays up to a year, extendable up to three years, without specific income requirements (Goats On The Road).

- Asia: In Asia, countries like Thailand, Malaysia, and Bali (Indonesia) are popular for digital nomads. Although specific "digital nomad visas" are still developing, these countries offer various long-term visa options suitable for remote work (Nomad Girl).

- Europe: Europe leads in digital nomad visas, with over twenty countries offering such programs. Estonia, Germany, Portugal, and Malta have well-established digital nomad visas. For instance, Portugal's visa allows remote workers to stay for up to a year, renewable for up to five years (Nomad Capitalist).

These visas typically require proof of stable income, health insurance, and sometimes a clean criminal record. The requirements and benefits vary, so it's essential to check the specific details for each country.

TruNorth Wealth Management, LLC
1662 HWY 395 N, Suite 203
Minden, NV 89423

Phone: 775-364-0010
Website: www.TruNorthWealth.com

Danette Lowe, CFP®
Email: Danette@TruNorthWealth.com

Securities offered through Registered Representatives of Cambridge Investment Research, Inc., a broker-dealer, member FINRA/SIPC. Advisory services offered through Cambridge Investment Research Advisors, Inc., a Registered Investment Advisor. TruNorth Wealth Managment and Cambridge are not affiliated. Cambridge does not offer tax or legal advice. Fixed insurance services offered through TruNorth Wealth Management.

This material is intended for informational/educational purposes only and should not be construed as tax or legal advice, investment advice, a solicitation, or a recommendation to buy or sell any security or investment product. You should consult a financial, legal or tax professional regarding your individual situation.

Diversification does not assure a profit or protect against loss in declining markets.

Environmental, social, and governance (ESG) criteria is based on a set of nonfinancial principles in addition to financial principles used to evaluate potential investments. The incorporation of nonfinancial principles (i.e., ESG) can factor heavily into the security selection process. The investment's ESG focus may limit investment options available to the investor.

Investments are subject to risk, including the loss of principal. Some investments are not suitable for all investors, and there is no guarantee that any investing goal will be met.

The case studies in this book are for illustrative purposes and should not be construed as a recommendation. It may not be representative of your experience.

Danette Gay Lowe, CFP®

I began my career as a Financial Advisor in 1999, embarking on a journey that has seen me guide clients through some of the most challenging times in the financial markets, including the dot-com crash, the credit crisis, and the recent global pandemic. As a CERTIFIED FINANCIAL PLANNER™ practitioner and the founder of TruNorth Wealth Management, I've dedicated myself to helping pre-retirees navigate complex financial landscapes with resilience and foresight.

My approach to retirement planning focuses on building sustainable income streams that can weather inflation and market fluctuations. Beyond financial security, I believe in preparing for retirement holistically, ensuring that my clients can live fully and purposefully during their retirement years.

Personally, I'm driven by the common obstacles I see people face. Too often, individuals delay retirement because their identities are tied to their careers or they fear financial constraints. I'm passionate about dispelling these myths and encouraging people to start exploring their passions now, integrating these into their lives to pave the way for a fulfilling retirement.

In addition to my financial advisory work, I've founded Shine First Today, a passion project aimed at helping individuals overcome anxiety and panic attacks. Through this initiative and my podcast "Shine First Today," I provide practical tools and insights to enhance mental well-being and productivity.

In "The Early Start Retirement Plan," I invite you to visualize the possibilities of how to spend your time, based on the things you're passionate about. By sharing inspirational stories and practical strategies, I empower you to begin your retirement planning journey with confidence. My goal is to expand your horizons, demonstrate the myriad possibilities available in retirement, and encourage you to craft a future that resonates with your deepest aspirations.

Thank you for reading! I invite you to reach out to me directly at: **danette@trunorthwealth.com**

I personally answer all emails and would love to hear your feedback, thoughts, and stories about your own retirement planning journey.

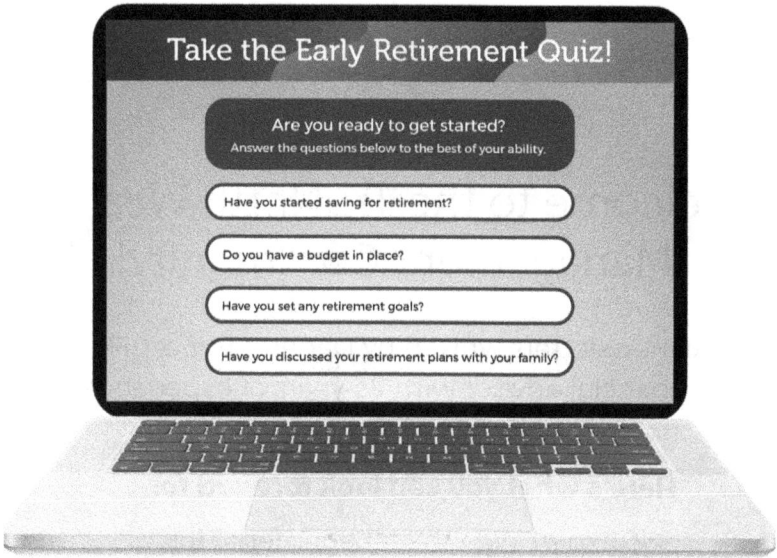

Take the Early Retirement Quiz!

Are you ready to get started?
Answer the questions below to the best of your ability.

Have you started saving for retirement?

Do you have a budget in place?

Have you set any retirement goals?

Have you discussed your retirement plans with your family?

Ready to Assess Your Retirement Readiness?

Take our simple Retirement Readiness Quiz to see how prepared you are for your future!

✔ Gain insights into your current retirement planning.

✔ Identify areas where you can improve.

✔ Get actionable tips to enhance your retirement strategy.

Start now and take the first step towards a secure and fulfilling retirement!

TAKE THE QUIZ
Scan the QR code to take the quiz today!

Welcome to the TruNorth Wealth Management Community!

All newsletters written by Danette Lowe, CFP®
a financial advisor with 25 years of experience!

Here's what you can look forward to:

✔ Expert Wealth Management Tips

✔ Retirement Planning Guidance

✔ Mindfulness in Finance

✔ Exclusive Podcast Updates

Join us today and take the first step towards a more informed, mindful, and secure financial future.

Your journey to financial wellness starts here.

WHEN YOU SIGN UP YOU'LL RECEIVE:
The 3 Steps to Planning an Epic Retirement Workbook

SIGN UP NOW
Scan the QR code to visit my site and subscribe to the newsletter today!

Check out my podcast!

In each of our Ready to Retire podcast episodes, Danette shares free resources, and easy-to-understand materials about retirement planning. These episodes will help to enhance and enrich your life, no matter your age, income, or retirement preparation level.

LISTEN NOW
Scan the QR code to start
listening to my podcast today!

www.ingramcontent.com/pod-product-compliance
Lightning Source LLC
Chambersburg PA
CBHW070656190326
41458CB00052B/6904/J